Rhoda Broughton

Scylla or Charybdis?

A Novel

Rhoda Broughton

Scylla or Charybdis?
A Novel

ISBN/EAN: 9783337027728

Printed in Europe, USA, Canada, Australia, Japan

Cover: Foto ©Thomas Meinert / pixelio.de

More available books at **www.hansebooks.com**

SCYLLA OR CHARYBDIS?

SCYLLA OR CHARYBDIS?

A NOVEL

BY

RHODA BROUGHTON

AUTHOR OF NANCY, SECOND THOUGHTS, A BEGINNER, ETC.

NEW YORK
D. APPLETON AND COMPANY
1895

SCYLLA OR CHARYBDIS?

CHAPTER I.

"This must be the house, William! This must be the house!"

Until it had pulled up at her door, the occupant of a bow window, projecting over the street, had not suspected that a landau, which has been making its way with horses kept to a walk and footman uncertainly consulting the faces of succeeding domiciles, had any visiting intention toward herself. No sooner has she realized this fact and the other one, that a voice and a parasol are waving and shouting directions from inside, than she slips noiselessly off the cushioned window-seat running round the embrasure, into the interior of the summer-darkened room. Mrs. Clarence is a shy woman, and she has not recognized either the voice, the parasol, or the liveries. She is a shy woman,—a good deal retired from the world,—and she awaits with some slight trepidation the outcome of the incident.

"It is probably the wrong house," she says to herself.

But this explanation is disproved by the fact that the footman's resounding rap is followed shortly by an undoubted admittance, by a strange step on the stairs, and by the parlor maid's announcement of a splendid rustling, châtelaine-clattering "Lady Bramshill." To the modest mouse-color-clad lady upon whom it is sprung, the title is as unfamiliar as the rest of the vision.

"Why do not you have your number on your door?" asks the intruder, in a loudish but not disagreeable voice. "How is one to find you out?"

"I am very sorry, but they are renumbering the street—changing the numbers. I do not quite know why."

"I asked which was No. 22 at the White Hart, and the secretary said she did not know, but the hall-porter would. I asked the hall porter, and he said he did not know, but the policeman would. I asked the policeman, and he said he did not know, but that the milkman would. I asked the milkman—or, at least, I made William, my footman, ask him—and he said he did not know, but that the postman would. I asked the postman—and, *enfin*, I am here!"

Mrs. Clarence has thought her visitor's opening speech as tiresome as her appearance at all is unaccounted for.

"It is evident that I am not much known to fame in St. Gratian," she replies, with a shy smile and an inward hope that her face does not betray her total ignorance of her visitor's identity. But that hope is not long left to her.

"You have not the foggiest idea who I am," says that visitor good-humoredly, but not even attempting to give her remark an interrogatory shape.

"Well, I cannot return the left-handed compliment, for I certainly should have known you anywhere."

"Should you?" with a distressed and timid glance at the portly and prosperous expanse before her, as if to evoke thereby some helpful memory; but none such comes, and she can only murmur: "*Lady Bramshill.*"

The other laughs.

"That will not help you. My name is as new as my gloves, which I put on to do you honor—and much too small they are! I cannot imagine why the shops have altered all the sizes! It is not three months since my judge was given a peerage."

My judge! The visitor is, then, the wife of a dignitary of the law. But Mrs. Clarence scans the horizon of her narrow acquaintance in vain. No judge rises, beneficent and rescuing, upon it.

"I think he appeared on the scene after you had left Green Leigh."

At the mention of this name—that of a place which she had quitted a quarter of a century ago, and where she had spent the five years of her wifehood—a place even more infinitely remote in the spirit's calendar than in that of the body—Mrs. Clarence gives a slight start.

"Life is a system of compensations," continues Lady Bramshill cheerfully; "he rose on my horizon as you disappeared over it. As soon as I was married I went to India. We did not come back, except to put the children to school, until last year. Have you any glimmering of a notion as to who I am *now?*"

A pleased confidence in an immediate joyous recognition following upon these indications is legibly written across her features, and upon Mrs. Clarence's memory there rises the cloudy figure of a big-framed, thin young woman, the bustling eldest of the Vicarage brood at her gates—a young woman of her own age, who, in that immeasurable distance, had served her as friend. But the outline is still so nebulous that her visitor has time for a look of disappointment and a rather crestfallen "I know that I have expanded a good deal," before the person to whom she seems to herself to have disclosed so unmistakably her personality proffers hesitatingly, in a faint and dubious key :

"*Not* Marion Baynes?"

"You make me doubt my own identity when you question it in that voice!" cries Lady Bramshill, with a touch of good-humored mortification. "Am I, then, so absolutely unrecognizable? Why, I should have known you to be Lucy Clarence anywhere."

"Ah, but you must remember what an advantage you had over me!" replies the other, in distressed apology. "You were expecting to see me, while I—— No doubt if I had been prepared for our meeting, I, too, should——"

But the fib dies on her lips. Under no circumstances of preparation could she have extracted from the plethoric and diamond-earringed area before her the scraggy form of the comrade of her early matronhood.

"I dare say you will find that my *in*side is not as much changed as my *out*side," says the area, with a philosophic laugh at her quondam friend's vain attempt. "It was by the merest chance that I learned

you were living here. I was in Deane's shop,—
the draper in Abbey Street, you know,—and I heard
one of the shopmen say to another, 'Has Mrs. Clarence's mantle been sent home?' I pricked up my
ears at once, for it is not a common name : you are
the only Clarence I know of without a 'Fitz.'"

"Am I?"

"I immediately began to question him about you,
and when I found that you were a widow lady, with
dark hair and eyes, and only lately come to the town,
I thought I had enough to go upon to justify my trying to find out whether you were *my* Mrs. Clarence.
But what a chance it was!"

"Yes, quite a chance!"

"He told me"—speaking more slowly and doubtfully—"that he thought you lived *alone*."

Her eyes have wandered round the room as if to
gather indications as to the truth or falsehood of this
fact, and come back with a sort of apprehension to
her hostess' face.

"I am alone most of the day, and I am alone just
now; but my son lives with me."

"Your son?" (drawing a long breath of relief).
"Oh, thank goodness that is all right! I was almost
afraid to ask. Such dreadful things happen to people,
and when the shopman said that you lived alone, I
thought—I feared that he might—might be——"

"Oh, do not suggest it!" interrupts the mother,
with a sort of cry, her natural gentleness conquered
by the superstitious impulse to avert the dread word
hovering on her questioner's lip. "Should I be here
if he were? What have I to live for but him?"

In answer to this ejaculation the visitor gives a sort of friendly, dissentient grunt, while her look travels with significant admiration over the still eminently charming form before her; the slight figure, on which the baleful *elderly spread* has not yet laid its thickening hand; the close-grained, petal-textured skin, the fine abundance of the inky hair, and the pathos of the antelope eyes.

"H'm! I should think you had as much to live for as most women, though why you should elect to live here——"

"It is very quiet," replies the other, recovering the restful softness of her normal manner, and looking a little ashamed of her unusual outbreak, "and I do not know anyone here. Of course,"—with a pretty, pensive smile, which shows her admiring and a little envious coeval that her teeth are in as good repair as the rest of the fabric,—"old friends are different, but I do not wish to make new acquaintances."

"Why not, in Heaven's name?"

"I have lived so long out of the world that I have lost the habit of it. If you remember"—a slight curve of the fine cheek which only needs development to become another smile—"I never had much to say. Well, now I have *nothing!*"

"If you went out more, you would soon find plenty; my difficulty is"—laughing—"that I always have too much. Well, after all"—jollily—"it is a fault on the right side. But what does your boy say to your shutting yourself up?"

"*My boy?*" with a tinge of proud amusement. "Do you know how old and how big my boy is?"

"Of course I cannot say as to his size, but how old?"—musingly—"why, good Heavens! he must be eight-and-twenty. It is five-and-twenty years since you left Green Leigh, and he was three years old then."

"Yes, he is eight-and-twenty."

"Good Heavens!" with another and yet more astounded glance at the slender outline and the dark hair, "it is incredible! you are a walking fraud upon society!"

"And he is always there to show me up."

There is such profound and joyful pride underlying the soft playfulness of the complaint that the idea strikes Lady Bramshill that either her long-lost friend's son must be an uncommonly fine young man, or that her besotment passes the bounds allotted to parental partiality.

"And he lives with you?"

"He comes down most evenings."

"From London?"

"Yes."

"Has he a profession?"

"He has just been called to the bar. I expect him back to-day"—with an involuntarily wistful peep at the clock—"from his first circuit."

"Is not it rather hard to work the Law Courts from here?"

"It is only an hour and a half from door to door."

"I should live in London if I were you."

"Should you?"

"Or what do you say to the suburbs?"

"We neither of us like the idea of the suburbs."

"But surely it is very bad for him to have three hours of train every day of his life."

"Do you think so?" anxiously. "But, then, he gets into fresher air."

"Why not live quite in the country?"

"He thinks it would be so lonely for me."

"But do you not know anyone here?"

"No."

"Then, it must be quite as lonely to you as Salisbury Plain."

Thus driven into a corner, and with her own and her son's want of reasoning powers so irrefragably demonstrated to her, Mrs. Clarence is meekly silent.

"I am afraid you will not like it when you get to know it, either; there is really nothing to recommend it; it is a perfect Sleepy Hollow."

"Perhaps that is its recommendation to me. I am rather sleepy, too."

"The churches of course are beautiful, architecturally, and I believe the choirs are good; but one cannot live on oriel windows and Gregorian chants."

"I should be sorry to try, but I like the services."

"Oh, you are *churchy*, are you?" in a tone of good-humored discontent.

"Your accent"—with a low laugh—"says that *you* are not!"

"Well, of course I ought to be—a parson's daughter, and all that; but I suppose it is a case of the grocer's boy and the raisins. I remember now that you were always inclined to be a saint in the old days."

"*I?*"

"Yes, *you! you!* In a quiet way, I mean, and with no blowing of trumpets. My father always said so, and in his day he was reckoned rather an authority, though they would think small-beer enough of him now. My father dead? Oh, yes, bless you! years ago, and so are most of my brothers and sisters; in fact, I should be lonely and dismal enough if I had not happily made plenty of new ties "—relapsing into cheerfulness—"plenty, indeed, with a vengeance!"

"You mean that you have children?"

For answer the visitor lifts the gloved hands of whose tightness she had complained, and, holding them up, expands the fingers.

"I am ashamed to pronounce the word, but that is the number: nine male and one female hostages to fortune, not counting the judge."

"*Ten?*"

"Yes, ten! The one female hostage is sitting outside in the carriage at this moment. I would not let her come in, because I thought that if it were not you she should not witness my discomfiture, and that if it *were* you, she would be in the way."

"Will not she come in?" asks Mrs. Clarence, with shy hospitality. "May I send down and ask her to come in? Is she—grown up?"

"She is five feet seven and a half"—proudly—"and only just turned eighteen; a very pretty girl, too, though I say it that should not—not that I ever see why one should not. But do not send for her; we do better without her, and I hope you will have many opportunities of cultivating her acquaintance;

or if your curiosity about her is very lively, peep at her between the slats of your Venetian blinds. By the by, why do you have Venetians? they are always getting out of order. Why not those nice matting ones instead?"

In obedience to the mother's suggestion, Mrs. Clarence peeps downward as directed between the slats of the Venetians. Then she draws back her neck.

"She is extremely pretty," is her comment. It is polite, but the parent detects a want of enthusiasm.

"Of course it is not a becoming angle to look at anyone from; the top of her hat and the tip of her nose do not give a quite adequate idea of her, but she *is* pretty! Whom she got it from, who shall say?"—with a laugh. "It is one of those mysterious throw-backs, I suppose, but she *is*. It is such a mercy that she is the girl. The nine boys are all one plainer than another."

"*Nine!*"

"Yes, *nine!* We ran rather short of Christian names toward the end, and we have overstocked all the professions; however, it is a fault on the right side. It is safer than having everything in one boat. But I ought not to say that to you, ought I? I have no doubt that your one boat is perfectly seaworthy. Is he strong—quite strong? I have a sort of recollection of your spending one whole summer away from home at the seaside; was that—what a slippery eel memory is!—was that for his health?"

"No, oh, no! he has always been quite well and strong."

"To be sure, I remember now; it was before he was born. And so he has never given you any anxiety on that head?"

"Nor on any other"—with a low fervency.

"What a mercy for you! He is not married?"

"No!" with a start.

"Ah, that is a pleasure to come! But, perhaps"—reassuringly—"it will not come—or at least, not yet awhile. Let him smoke all over the house, and perhaps it will not come at all."

"He is twenty-eight years old," says the mother, with a slight tremble in her voice, "and he has never shown the slightest preference for anyone."

"Hasn't he? How very odd! When he does take the disease, how badly he will——"

She breaks off, her good-natured if inquisitive eye realizing by the look on her friend's face what very little enjoyment she is deriving from her prognostics.

"I dare say that as long as he has you he will not wish for Venus herself. I suppose"—with a glance of kindly admiration at her hostess' severely simple, yet dainty-detailed, toilet—"that it is for him, since you say that you have given up the world, that you are so beautifully *soignée*."

"He likes me to look neat."

"You always cared for your clothes; that was my chief misgiving when I came here. I thought that the Mrs. Clarence who would buy a mantle at Deane's shop could not be *you*."

"It was not for myself," replies the other, with a slight smile at the rightness of her friend's intuition; "it is for a little cousin who is coming to stay with me, and who, living in the depths of the country, will think anything that comes out of a shop beautiful."

"A girl cousin?" raising her eyebrows, and in a tone which, did she weigh half a dozen stone less, would be called "arch." "How rash!"

But since, once again, at this would-be pleasantry, the look of distress which, with one so gentle, takes the place of anger, clouds her hostess' face, Lady Bramshill goes off on a new line:

"But do not let us waste time in making jokes" (the visitee's conscience acquits her of any such velleity), "and let us talk about the past—about poor dear old Green Leigh."

"It is let," replies the other, with quiet brevity, and not showing any expansive desire to enlarge upon her answer.

"Ah! I supposed so. On a long lease?"

"Twenty-one years, which expired four years ago, and then my son renewed it."

"You have no intention of going back, then?"

"None."

"I do not wonder; still, it is, or was, a sweet pretty place." To this expression of admiration Mrs. Clarence neither assents, nor does she dissent from it; and her friend has to take the thread up again herself: "Still, I can, of course, perfectly understand your feelings." Mrs. Clarence's movements are all very gentle, but she stirs uneasily. It is evident that, whatever the feelings alluded to may be, she has no desire for sympathy in, or reviving of, them. "Yes, I can quite understand your feelings; but we will not talk of painful things, will we? even though it is such a long-ago pain as Green Leigh"—with a slight streak of surprise. "What I want to know, and what I dare say you will not mind telling me, is what has been happening to you all these years since the P. and O. boat steamed me out of your orbit."

Mrs. Clarence looks dreamily round the room, as if seeking for a good, plump, bouncing event to offer her questioner. But apparently she finds none, for she answers:

"I do not think that anything has happened."

"*Nothing happened in twenty-five years!*"

Thus crudely presented, Mrs. Clarence's assertion does sound both ridiculous and incredible, and she is shamefacedly conscious of it.

"I mean," she says, faintly coloring, "that nothing that matters seems to have happened—nothing outside ourselves. We have led a very retired life, and the years have slidden past us without taking much notice of us. No,"—smiling more decidedly,—"I cannot conscientiously say that in the last quarter of a century anything has happened, except that Harry has grown up."

"Harry! How glad I am that you have mentioned his name. I could not recall it, and was ashamed to ask. Harry! Have I a Harry? Of course I have! You could not mention a Christian name of which I have not a specimen! Harry! I wonder why you called him Harry?" But here, again, the person interpellated has apparently no reason to offer, or, at all events, offers none. "When you left Green Leigh you settled—where?"

"I lived at Margate for six years."

"What on earth possessed you to do that?"

"On account of the air."

"I suppose you had had a complete nervous breakdown?"

"No, I had not; it was not for myself."

"For your boy? But you say that he has always been perfectly strong."

"So he has; but I thought it would be a good thing to have him well braced up before going to school."

"Oh, you did make up your mind to send him to school! where?"

"He was at a preparatory school at Folkestone till he went to Eton."

"And you?"

"I took a house at Sandgate, to be near him."

"And when he went to Eton did you stay on at Folkstone?"

"No; I moved to Windsor."

The visitor is seized with a sort of good-humoredly derisive chuckle at this last answer.

"What a convenient thing to have only one chick! I should have had to be cut into a good many pieces if I had followed all my lads to school. Wellington, Sandhurst, Rugby, Radley; it would have been a case of, 'Give every town a limb!' And when he left Eton?"

"He went to Oxford."

"And you—you went to Oxford, too?"

"Yes."

Lady Bramshill breaks into an uncontrollable laugh.

"My dear Lucy! Not really? I never heard of any boy's parents, except Ruskin's, chaperoning him through his university course."

"Did not you?"

"And did you escort him to his lectures and his wines?"—still laughing.

"I do not think that I made him ridiculous"—very quietly, though an intimate, if she had one, might detect an accent of mortification. "He was at New; he did not live with me. He only came to see me when he had a spare half-hour."

Perhaps, though no longer an intimate, the visitor divines that the rough rallying which is of such frequent and successful employ among her own robust and unsensitive brood is out of place in this shy hermitage.

"And when he left Oxford he read for the bar; and you—happily for me, and unhappily for you—set up your tent-pole in this dreary little country town? I know all about you *now*. Now it is your turn! Ask me any and every question you feel inclined about myself and my judge, and my nine ugly boys and my one pretty girl! She *is* pretty,"—with a streak of pique,—"though I know you do not believe it."

"Oh, but indeed I do!" distressed. "From the glimpse I caught of her, I thought her very, *very* pretty!"

Had Lady Bramshill suspected what a tribute to her daughter's charms was implied by the faintness of Mrs. Clarence's encomiums—Mrs. Clarence, to whom a pretty girl is an object of shrinking terror, the occasion of putting to herself afresh the agonized question in her heart's depths, "Is it she who is to deal me my deathblow?"—her mother's vanity would have been satisfied, even without the second and stronger testimony which she has forced. Now, content with saying :

"Wait till you see her in the evening," she goes on : "Ask me anything you feel inclined about us ; I do not care where you begin. We have no skeleton closets."

Nothing can be handsomer or more liberal than the terms of the permission ; but the person to whom it is given seems at first incapable of availing herself of it. Between a nervous fear of asking amiss and a guilty consciousness of her own lack of any real interest in the past history of her long-lost-sight-of, and, to say the truth, absolutely forgotten friend, she hesitates so obviously that the friend has to go to her rescue.

"One does not quite know where to begin. It will all come out presently in bits ; and you have not my cheek—rushing into your past like a bull into a china shop. It is a comfort to think that there is no hurry ; that, since you are here—I really cannot imagine why—we shall have endless opportunities of meeting."

"Yes"—rather faintly.

"Have you a carriage? No? Then, I will come or send for you ; and, if I happen not to be able to do either,—we are not very well horsed just now,—I may tell you that they have very good flys at the White Hart ; only mind that you do not let them charge you four miles—it is not a yard more than three and a half to The Beeches."

If a certain weak sinking of the heart at this revelation of the near neighborhood of her garrulous companion, and of the only-just-seen-enough-to-be-alarmed-at white nose tip and pink straw hat in the carriage below, is perceptible to herself in Mrs. Clarence's soul at this hearty speech, she at least gives no outward sign of it.

"The Beeches!" she repeats civilly. "Is that your house? What a pretty rural name!"

"We are just beginning to get it into shape. You must come and help us; you had always a great deal of taste, and I see"—with a glance at the arrangement of the low and unassuming but graceful room—"that you have not lost it. Give us an early day, and we will show you all our Indian things."

This last promise produces a further inward declension of the listener's spirits.

"Thank you."

"Not that it is easy to get anything pretty in India now; aniline dyes and American taste have played the deuce with those colors which used to be so wonderfully harmonious. The judge cannot get over it."

"Cannot he?"

"He says that it is inconceivable what a change in that respect there is since he first went to India. But, to be sure, that must be nearly fifty years ago! One must expect a good many changes in fifty years."

"Yes, one must."

"Though *you*"—with a smile—"say that nothing has happened to you in half that time."

"Did I say so? It was silly of me; but I meant nothing *vital*."

"Well, I suppose I must be going now, or Euphemia will be getting restive."

"Is Euphemia your girl's name?"

"Yes—at last you have found a question to ask; you know, the judge is Scotch—Euphemia! And I would not have it shortened into Effie."

"No!"

"But before I go we *must* fix upon a day and hour for you to come to us—you and your Harry. No, do not be afraid, I will not call him Harry to his face; I know how young men hate to be Christian-named by old women!"

Mrs. Clarence hesitates.

"It is very kind of you, but I am afraid I cannot quite answer for him."

"I thought you said that he was coming home to-day?"

"Yes, I expect him; but—but you know he goes up to London every day to the Temple."

"The law courts do not sit in August."

Thus a second time convicted of falsehood and folly, Mrs. Clarence remains helplessly silent, and her antagonist pushes her advantage.

"He is sure to be at home to-morrow?"

"I do not know; he has not said so."

"Let us say to-morrow on the chance; we lunch at two, and the carriage shall be at this door precisely at 1.30."

But despite the excessive meekness of her look, it is now apparent that Mrs. Clarence is capable of holding her own.

"It is most kind of you to be in such a hurry to have us," she answers courteously, "but I could not possibly answer for Harry. If you will allow me, I will write."

"Wire—we have a telegraph and telephone in the house; trust an old Indian for making himself comfortable. But do let it be 'yes.' Well, it has been pleasant picking up the old threads."

The serene and civil mask of Lady Bramshill's friend's face gives no indication of how shudderingly repellant to her is the occupation alluded to, and her sweet enigmatic parting smile may mean acquiescence as well as gratitude.

CHAPTER II.

LADY BRAMSHILL has stepped, heavy-footed, but excited and kiss-blowing, into her landau, and it has rolled away with her and Euphemia.

"If you had stayed five minutes longer, I should have screamed," is the young lady's opening remark.

"Was I so long?" apologetically. "I hope you did not mind waiting?"

"Of course I minded. I was excessively bored. But was it she—was it your old friend?"

"Oh, yes, yes!"

"I thought it must be by your staying so long. But I *am* surprised. I had no doubt of your being shown the door."

"No more had I—at least, not much; but the moment I saw her I knew it was all right. I should have known her anywhere; I told her so."

"And she? Did she return the compliment?"

"Well, no, I cannot say that she did; in fact, she did not know me from Adam."

"You must remember"—with a rather mischievous glance at her parent's outline—"that you always tell me you were a thin girl."

"So I was; and then the name, of course, was no clew."

"Our 'new nobility' is perhaps a little misleading," replies Euphemia, laughing.

"But as soon as I mentioned Green Leigh, or almost as soon, she recollected me at once."

"And fell upon your neck?"

"No; she never was a very demonstrative person."

"But she was delighted to see you?"

"Oh, yes, of course—at least,"—as if the idea had struck her for the first time—"now that I come to think of it, was she? She did not say so; but, then, she never was demonstrative. She *has* worn well"—returning to a branch of the subject on which confidence is easier; "a wonderful woman! such a pretty creature still!"

"*Pretty* at fifty?"

"Not fifty—forty-seven."

"Forty-seven, fifty, it is all the same."

The mother does not waste time in contesting the fiat of cruel and magnificent eighteen, but continues her pæan of praise.

"And so beautifully turned out! all thrown away upon a wretched little country town! Why she came here I cannot make out; and she herself did not seem very clear. I shall never rest till I get her out of it."

"I suppose she knows her own business best," rejoins Euphemia shrewdly; "I think, if I were you, I would leave her to manage it; you know that people are not always quite pleased when you insist on rearranging their lives for them."

"I do not know what you mean," rejoins Lady Bramshill, with a warmth which shows that there may be some basis in fact for the accusation, "but I shall never be satisfied till I get them out of this *hole!*" with a contemptuous glance at the clean but lifeless street through which they are rolling countryward.

"*Them?* I thought that she was a widow."

"So she is, but she has a son."

"A son? What is he like?"

"I did not see him, he was not there; but he is to return to-day, and I begged them both to come over at once."

"And what day are they coming?"

"I do not know. I could not get her to fix any day; she made rather a difficulty about him: could not answer for him—that sort of thing. A little absurd, I thought."

"Well, you know you would not dare to answer for me," rejoins the young lady, laughing, "so perhaps he is a tyrant of the same stamp."

"She seemed to imply that he was a monstrous fine fellow, and if he takes after her, he may be. Well, I have no doubt we shall see plenty of him when once we meet. I wonder "—with a laugh of ill-contained pride—" whether poor dear Lucy was afraid of my throwing you at her prodigy's head!"

"Did such an idea cross your mind?" asks the girl, with cool interest. "But no, match-maker as you are, the scale of the establishment did not promise much of a *parti*, and 'us nobility' must look high; yet," as her mother does not immediately answer, "you are romantic enough to have entertained the thought for a moment, too, though I do you the justice to believe you would hasten to dismiss it."

Lady Bramshill shakes her head.

"Poor dear Lucy! No,"—reflectively, yet very decidedly, too,—"she may indeed make her mind easy! Not for even one second—not even in joke—should I be likely to contemplate such a possibility, or, rather," with great emphasis, "such an *im*possibility."

"Why an impossibility? Did their grandfather, like Sydney Smith's, disappear about the time of the assizes? Is there any dark spot in your friend's history!"

"In *hers?* Oh, no; she was always a perfect Sainte Nitouche—a little angel, who was only held to earth by the one thread of a slight weakness for her clothes."

"The husband, then? Was there anything wrong about him?" Lady Bramshill nods. "He drank?" No answer. "Your silence says, 'like a fish,' though I always think that that expression is rather hard upon fish, who are such rigid Blue-Ribbons."

"He was a harmless sort of dull man in his normal state; but when he was—ill——"

"D. T., of course?"

"I never said D. T."—sharply. "He used to knock her about cruelly. I have seen bruises an inch long on her neck and arms; and once he cut her forehead open with a medicine bottle; I saw the little white scar under her hair to-day."

"And I suppose she used to fly for refuge to the Vicarage—it was only just across the park, was it not?—to you and my grandfather?"

"Not she! She never breathed a word upon the subject to any living soul, except one woman servant, who helped her to nurse him. By the bye, I wonder has she that woman, that Mrs. Nasmyth, still? It was a perfect marvel how she managed to keep people ignorant of what really ailed him; but she did, and even when he had to be sent away from home nobody suspected it. People thought he had been ordered to Kissingen. God knows how she managed it; but that woman, in her little fragile body, has the pluck of the devil!"

"She must indeed!"—with an accent of sincere admiration—"but I do not think you ought to say 'the pluck of the devil.' It is not ladylike."

"No, I suppose I ought not," rejoins the mother dutifully. "Thank you, dear, for telling me; but, really, when I think of what a hell upon earth that poor little woman must have borne in unflinching silence and endurance——"

"If she kept it so dark, how did you discover it?"

"It oozed out after his death—after she had left the neighborhood. By the bye, I expect that the knowledge that it must come out sooner or later had a good deal to say to her letting the place. She naturally thought that the knowledge of such a parentage would injure the boy."

"Why on earth should it? How grossly unjust if it did?" cries Euphemia, with a generous flush of indignation on her pink-velvet face. "To be cold-shouldered because he had had a drunken brute for a father—impossible!"

"I never mentioned the word 'drink,' and you do not know what you are talking about," rejoins Lady Bramshill, with more brusqueness than she is wont to employ toward her daughter, impelled by who knows what lurking fear aroused by this hot partisanship. "The poor wretch was not at all responsible. But it is a very disagreeable subject; do not let us dwell upon it."

The daughter receives this request in silence, while her eyes rest thoughtfully on the passing hedges, dark and dusty with the August thirst, for the town has been left behind, the bridge over its slow river crossed, and backs turned upon its soaring spires; but that her mother's injunctions are not invariably binding upon her is proved by her next remark:

"I can quite see why Mrs. Clarence was not as glad to see you as you expected."

"I never said that she was not glad to see me"—hastily interjected, but not paid much attention to.

"The poor woman has for all these years been trying to bury that hideous past, and, of course, the first sight of you dug it all up again. You will probably find that she has flitted early to-morrow morning."

"I do not know why you should say that," replies Lady Bramshill, in a distinctly wounded voice. "If she remembers me at all—and I must say she did seem strangely hazy about me—she—she must know that I am the last person in the world to peach upon her; that I would bite my tongue out sooner than not keep her counsel. My one thought to-day, ever since I first saw her sitting on that window-seat, looking out into that dead-alive street, was how I could make a brighter existence for her."

"I would not try, if I were you."

"I *must* get her back into the world—wake her up—make her feel her own value."

"I repeat that, if I were you, I would not try. As long as I have known you you have always been trying to make chickens swim and ducklings fly, and somehow it has never quite come off."

. . . . .

Could the eyes of the interlocutors traverse the intervening two miles, and pierce the old brick of Mrs. Clarence's house-wall, they would see, to the daughter's triumph and the mother's discomfiture, that the surmises of the former had been more correct than the not very confident hopes of the latter. No sooner are Lady Bramshill and her india-rubber-tired landau beyond the reach of parting smiles and out of the range of hand-kissing, than the object of her endearments sinks down in an armchair, and, knitting together her small, long hands, says to herself over and over, in a voice of unmistakable distress, "How unfortunate! Oh, *how* unfortunate!"

But after a while her thoughts apparently return to the pleasanter channel from which they had been diverted by her unwelcome visitor, for she rises and, slightly shaking her head, as if thereby to shake out of it the disagreeable train of thought awakened by Lady Bramhill's visit, she walks with, for her, an alert step—her movements are always soft and slow—back to the window-seat, and renews her watch down the street.

To the naked eye there is not much to look at in it, in its slumbrous afternoon quiet, half shade, half

August fire, deserted even by such gayety as the violent butcher boys and gentler greengrocers lend to its morning hours. It is chiefly composed of dwelling houses of the smaller gentry type—houses behind whose Liberty muslin blinds ancient gentlewomen, fragments of considerable families, are sitting, and solicitors and doctors are rearing their sprightly broods. The pavement is not actually grass-grown, but the sparrows have seldom to remove from its mid-cobbles—it is still paved with cobble-stones—in order to make way for a passing vehicle. It is, in fact, not a thoroughfare, but a most sleepy *cul-de-sac*. And yet, were it Piccadilly, the watcher's eyes could not be fixed with a more expectant eagerness upon its silent length, especially upon that end of it which communicates with the outer world.

Round that corner Harry will return from his first circuit. Rare indeed have been the occasions during his twenty-eight years of life when his mother has not herself opened the door to him on any return after absence, and acute has ever been her vexation when either illness, or the presence of any of her few visitors, or a change in her son's arrangements, has hindered her from being the first object on which his eyes fall on the threshold of his home. And if now, on this great epoch-making day, the return from this inauguration, as it were, of his career, he were to be admitted by a stupid parlor maid, who would see no special meaning in this return, what good would her life do her?

It is this fear which has added a sting to the thorn of Lady Bramshill's reminiscences—the fear lest the wheels of his hansom should be heard raising the echoes of St. Gratian while her old acquaintance is still keeping her on the gridiron of her recollections, and the alarmingly handsome young giantess-daughter is still leaning back under her gay parasol in the carriage outside.

But, thank Heaven! both are gone in plenty of time; for Mrs. Clarence has been upon her watchtower the best part of an hour, and that chronic fear of accidents under which all overmuch-loving persons are wont to suffer is beginning to beset her, when her spirits are sent up with a run by the sight of a gray horse, two big wheels, and a hansom-hooded form turning the expected angle.

To see her on the doorstep evidently causes her son no surprise, nor is there much overt emotion on either side in their salutations.

"Well, mother?"

"Well, dear?"

But after he has paid his cab, and followed her up the little old stairs to the shaded drawing room, she gives a long, low sigh of perfect satisfaction, and lays one gentle kiss—more might tease him—upon his stooped face.

He returns her caress fondly, asking, in a voice that sounds inspiritingly cheerful and manly in the unmanly room:

"Well, how have you been getting on? Not too dull?"

"Not dull at all. You know I like dullness; I am dull myself."

"I know you are"—with an intonation that takes

all sting out of the acquiescence—" at least, I ought to know it, for you have been telling me so for the last quarter of a century."

" And you ? " in a tone of suppressed excitement.

" What about me ? "

" Did you—did you get on all right ? "

" Yes, I think so ; as well as such a tender fledgling could expect."

" You enjoyed yourself ? "

" Extremely. I had a capital time. They are a very pleasant set of men on the Oxford Circuit. We had a most amusing mess."

" Yes ? "

" Hodgins—you have heard of him ? "

" I do not think so "—reluctantly.

" Oh, yes, you must ; only you have forgotten. He is a very coming man. He will probably take silk next year."

" Will he ? "

If there is any latent ignorance in Mrs. Clarence's mind of what soaring height of exaltation " taking silk " may mean, she is careful to give no indication of it.

" He is famous for his good stories. Many of them are too professional, too technical, for you to appreciate ; but I must tell you one or two that require no legal knowledge, and which I think will amuse you."

" I am sure they will."

" His *bon-mots* are renowned at the bar."

" Are they ? I suppose "—with great delicacy of hesitation—" that you did not get a brief ? It would have been most unlikely on your first circuit. I did not"—in hasty fear of the slightest implication of disappointment—"I did not in the least expect it."

She is looking with veiled eagerness in her son's face as she makes the disclaimer, and her spirits begin to flutter as she sees a smile dawning in his sea-blue eyes.

"Then you will be rather annoyed—one is always annoyed when one's previsions are falsified," he says, with a teasing slowness, in amused relish of her eager hanging on his utterance—"that I did get one. It was only by a fluke, I confess, and it was only one; but it was enough to take away my reproach among barristers."

"You did get one?" with a rapturous smile. "Oh, I am glad!"

"It was one of poor Hodgins'. It is an ill wind that blows nobody good. He was laid up with the gout at Oxford, and had to throw it up."

"Yes?"

"And so he gave it to me. He said—he is always so full of his jokes——"

"Even when he has the gout?" with a playful smile.

"Yes, even when he has the gout. He said, 'Which of you fellows looks the hungriest?'"

"I am sure"—indignantly—"that you do not look in the least hungry."

"I suppose he thought I did, for he gave it to me."

"And was it—was it a good case—an interesting one?"

"It was"—laughing—"an old woman, who brought an action against a tram company for knocking her down."

"Oh?" with a faintly disappointed intonation.

"She was not much hurt; but she was extremely angry, and determined to have very big compensation."

"And you got it for her? You won it?" her words tripping over each other in the eagerness of her inquiry.

"Yes, I won it; she got compensation and costs."

"Oh, I *am* pleased!"

"So was she."

"I should have liked to have seen your first brief. I suppose—do not laugh at me; no doubt I am saying something very stupid—I uppose you have not kept it? I see by your laughing that I am suggesting something impossibly silly."

"I am afraid that, as a rule, barristers do not lay up their briefs in lavender. They are not very interesting-looking documents; but I might get you a copy of mine."

"I should be very much obliged indeed to you if you would."

"When I am seated on the Woolsack, it will no doubt gain a market value," rejoins he, with a friendly jeer, walking as he speaks to the bow window, whence—the sun having for the day withdrawn his too potent smile—the Venetians have been drawn up. "Has one wheelbarrow passed up this gay thoroughfare since I left?" he asks, leaning out. "It is dead-alive, with a vengeance!"

She has joined him, and now stands with her hand on his shoulder. The identity of the epithet with that which her new acquaintance and old friend had applied to her chosen home striking her, she repeats :

"Dead-alive! It must be so, really, for you are the second person who has called it so this afternoon."

"Who was the first?"

"Lady Bramshill."

"Lady Bramshill!" withdrawing his head from the outer air and speaking with a slightly aroused interest. "What Lady Bramshill? Any relation to the Indian judge who was belorded at the last batch of promotions?"

"Only wife."

"And what made her rush into your acquaintance? Since you know no one here, how did she dig you out?"

"I knew her a great many years ago," replies Mrs. Clarence, with a sort of reluctance, though she herself had introduced the subject. "She was the daughter of the clergyman at Green Leigh. I did not know her under her married name; and she is so changed past all recognition that I should not have guessed her, even if she had kept her old one. People"—pensively putting her head on one side—"ought not to be hurt with one for not knowing them again, when they have lost all trace of likeness to their former selves."

"Was she hurt?"

"I am afraid so. She said pointedly that she should have known me anywhere, and that I was not in the least altered. That, of course, was nonsense."

"It is the best piece of sense I have yet heard of her. You are not in the least altered since first I knew you, and that is some little time ago," replies he, with a stoutness which proves that, whatever may be the intrinsic value of the opinion, he is ready to go to the stake for it. She throws a glance of fond and happy incredulity at him.

"Lady Bramshill brought her daughter with her."

"Her daughter! Whew-w!"

Perhaps the sort of whistle with which Harry Clarence concludes is due to some reminiscence that the possession of daughters is not apt to endear acquaintances to his parent.

"Yes; a very handsome daughter, so her mother says."

"And do you say so, too?" with a carefulness that might have amused a stranger, to throw no eagerness into the inquiry.

"I can scarcely judge. She did not come in; she sat in the carriage outside, the whole time. I could only see the top of her hat and a tiny bit of one cheek."

"So you keep your opinion in reserve, eh?"

"I do not think she was quite *your* style"—with a slight quickening of her slow, soft voice. "She is one of those endlessly long girls, taller than most men; and I know you do not admire giantesses."

"I detest them," replies he reassuringly. "The one thing that I could never forgive in a woman would be looking over my head. No," with a laughing, yet tender look at his mother's small stature, "give me a little woman, just as high as my heart."

CHAPTER III.

It is the morning of the third day after Harry Clarence's return. Lady Bramshill is sitting at her writing table, with the materials for a letter spread out before her, as she holds a suspended pen, with her eyes fondly resting on the neat new gilt coronet that has lately flowered out upon her stationery.

Her daughter is sitting near her on the arm of a sofa, with her legs, not dangling—there are few elevations from which Euphemia Bramshill's legs could dangle—but stretched out before her along the carpet.

"I am writing a line to Lucy Clarence to say that I shall send the carriage for them to-morrow—for her and her son. It must be the landau, because there is a cousin coming to stay with them; we must have the cousin, too. I am sure that must have been Harry Clarence, the tall man I told you I saw yesterday in the post office. Of course he will be only too glad to come; what can he have to do in St Gratian? Though *she* cannot answer for him, *I* can!" laughing. "But people say that kind of thing *pour se faire valoir!*"

"I wish you would not use quite so many French phrases," says Euphemia, in a key less of intentional disrespect than of dispassionate criticism. "Your accent is not very good."

"I have not had such advantages as you," replies her mother, without the least acrimony; "it is a silly trick, but they sometimes convey nicer shades of meaning than we can hit off."

"My Dear Lucy" (writing):

"I really cannot call her anything but Lucy. I hope she will not mind. She certainly cannot have any very pleasant associations with the name of Clarence, and we were always Lucy and Marion in old days."

"'My dear Lucy,'" says Euphemia, in laughing anticipatory parody of her mother's rather slowly-coming composition. "'The carriage shall be at your door at one o'clock to-morrow to convey reluctant you and your still-more-unwilling prodigy to my house to be introduced to my large and noisy family, whose acquaintance you have not the smallest desire to make.' I always think of you, mother, when I read the parable of the man who compelled people to come in that his house might be filled."

"Euphemia!" cries a vigorous young voice, which, with its owner, now enters the room with something of a burst, "here is a parcel for you, and I am sure by the shape it is your new cleik. Are not you ready yet? You said you would come golfing at eleven, and it is now half-past. We are all waiting for you."

"I am engaged," replies Euphemia rather loftily. "I will come presently; and meanwhile, my dear boy, I must beg you to enter a room more gently. It is not usual to storm into a lady's boudoir like a blizzard."

From her sofa-arm she waves him superbly away, and, though he is a full-grown youth, even a little her senior, he goes like a lamb, closing the door with the nicest precaution behind him.

Perhaps his docility mollifies the young autocrat, for she presently rises, as if to follow her brother, firing one parting shot at her parent, who has at length got under way with her note, which the daughter reads over her shoulder:

"'Send the carriage!' You may send the carriage, but I would wager a good deal that it returns empty."

. . . . .

"You have not heard any bad news?" asks Clarence, as he enters his mother's drawing room at luncheon-time, and finds her sitting with an open note on her lap, and her smooth head—she has had but one style of hair-dressing all her life: parting, thick silky sweep from the face, and large, low Greek knot—a good deal on one side. Long experience has taught him that to carry her head on one side is a sure signal of mental distress on his mother's part. At his approach it grows straight again.

"Any bad news, dear? No; why do you think I have had bad news?"

"You looked so woe-begone."

"Did I? I was only thinking."

"Thinking of what?"

"Of this," taking up the note and holding it out to him. "Lady Bramshill has just sent it over by a man on horseback. I cannot see," pensively, "that there was any such very great hurry about it."

The young man looks at sea for a moment, repeating "Lady Bramshill?" interrogatively; and, indeed, that lady's name has not been mentioned between them since the little conversation about her that had followed his arrival; but he takes the note and reads:

"'My Dear Lucy:'"

"Oh, I understand! it is your old friend; so you are on 'Lucy' terms!" slightly raising his eyebrows.

"'Now that we have found each other again, we must not let one another slip, but must make up for lost time. I cannot tell you how delightful it was to me yesterday to reknit the dear old tie and take up the long-dropped threads.'

"This good lady seems very fond of you."

Mrs. Clarence's head has, during the reading aloud of these sentences, been again declining considerably from the perpendicular, and she now ejaculates in a small and distressed voice:

"Yes, she was *so* much gladder to see me than I was to see her. Isn't it dreadful?"

"'Now, we must take time by the forelock, and as a first step I shall, if I do not hear from you to the contrary, or, indeed, even if I do, send the carriage to bring you and your Harry—tell him that I am almost sure I met him in the post office yesterday—and the girl cousin who, as you told me, is about to visit you, to luncheon, and spend a *long* day with us. I decline to take a "No."

"'Your truly attached old chum,

"'MARION BRAMSHILL.'"

"Well, and what have you said to 'your truly attached old chum'? That you are sorry to tell her you are not nearly so much attached as she?"

"I have not answered yet. I waited to consult you."

There is a little pause. He has sat down on a stool at her feet, and laid her letter back upon her knee. Then he speaks, rather hesitatingly, a suggestion that seems to be feeling its way doubtfully:

"You do not think that it would be a good thing if you came out of your shell a little bit—just a very, *very* little?"

"I should be as uncomfortable as any other limpet or scallop or poor shelled beast. But that is no reason, dear,"—speaking with a little eager hurry,—" why *you* should be cooped up with me; why you and Abigail should not accept the invitation. Lady Bramshill means very kindly,"—glancing remorsefully at the affectionate expressions which crowd her correspondent's page,—"and I dare say it is a pleasant house—full of cheerful young people. They are a large family; I do not know how many boys, and that one immensely tall girl—a very handsome girl, too!" she adds, afraid of there having been an ungenerous harping on what she knows to be in her son's eyes a disability in her speech.

"'If she be not fair for me, what care I how fair she be?' And you know I hate tall girls," replies he lightly. "As far as I am concerned, you have your answer pat, for I shall not be here. I forgot to tell you that I must be off to-morrow—only for a couple of nights!" seeing her efforts to conceal the fall in her barometer.

She has made it a lifelong rule not to question him as to his outgoings and incomings, and she now only says cheerfully:

"I hope it is something pleasant."

"I do not know. It is a *terra incognita* to me. I am going down to Eastshire."

"To stay with people?"

"To stay with a person."

"A new friend?"

"Well, I can hardly call Mrs. Bevis a friend yet, though I think she has the makings of one."

He pauses, and she waits patiently, without more questioning, for what enlargement on his announcement he may feel disposed to make.

"I met her first at one of those People's Concerts I went to sing at in the East End. She does some work there in connection with Toynbee Hall,—I think she has a good many irons in the fire, and that is one of them,—and we rather fraternized. We happened to meet again several times, and now she has asked me down to this little place she has in Eastshire. She describes it as a mere cottage. If you ask me," with a smile, "I am afraid it is not altogether admiration of my *beaux yeux* that dictated the invitation, but that she wants to consult me on a point of law as to a bit of land on which she is anxious to build a recreation room for her village."

Nothing can be plainer, opener, or less marked by the smallest tinge of embarrassment than this direct and simple relation, and Mrs. Clarence makes shift to receive it with an answering smile, but in her heart there is misliking of a project which is to house her son in a cottage in *tête-à-tête* with an—evidently by her invitation—enterprising female stranger. It occurs to her to say, in as *dégagé* a manner as she can master, "I should have thought that she would have had a lawyer of her own," but she crushes the impulse as implying a slight doubt of the propriety of the course adopted, and substitutes the innocent-looking remark:

"Mrs. Bevis! I do not remember her name. Is she a widow?"

"I imagine so. I never heard of a Mr. Bevis."

"Young or old?"

"I never know what age people are; but I do happen to know hers, for she mentioned last time I saw her—apropos of I forgot what—that she was forty."

A slight but insufficient breeze of relief blows in upon Mrs. Clarence's soul.

Forty! and Harry is twenty-eight; but, then, it is the mode of the day to marry your grandmother. She probes diffidently further:

"Nice-looking? What does she look like? I always"—apologetically—"wish to draw a picture to myself of your friends."

"Oh, she looks all right! I do not think either she or I trouble ourselves much about her looks."

The expression of indifference as to his hostess' charms is obviously sincere; and into the self-tormenting spirit of the mother there flows a (this time) full and ample stream of balm. Even to her ignorance of the world and of man it is patent that her Harry may be safely trusted even in a *tête-à-tête* in a thatched cottage with a lady whose beauties he can epitomize in the cool phrase, "Oh, she looks all right!"

It is therefore with unforced cheerfulness, and many injunctions not to hurry back on her account, that she smiles good-by to him from the doorstep. Anything sad or serious is further banished from her adieus by the fact that at the last moment but one the traveler's hatbox is missing, and in the little scuffle of finding it all other feelings are lost. She has never seen him leave her with less anxiety or foreboding, and yet——

Eastshire is a good distance from London, and August is not the picked month among months for pleasant traveling, particularly in the direction of the sea, near which the goal of Clarence's journey lies.

It is well on in the afternoon, after a four-mile drive in a fly—Mrs. Bevis has not sent to meet him; but, since he had not mentioned his train, he cannot blame her for the omission—that he finds himself at the door of her cottage. Since it is low, stands sociably close to the road, and has a deep-eaved roof, it may fairly be called so.

He is admitted by a very pretty parlor maid, in a Boulogne fish-wife's pleated cap, though her tongue betrays no Gallic tinge, and in whose whole air, though of accomplished politeness, he traces slight evidences of hurry and preoccupation. They are explained when he inquires for his hostess.

"She is in the harvest field, sir," with a faint sound of well-governed surprise at such a question being needful. "The cart, with the tea, is just going up there; perhaps you would like to go up in it?"

The young man hesitates. He would prefer a walk after his long sitting; but, reflecting that he does not know the way or the distance, he gratefully accepts the proposition, and in a few minutes, in company with the parlor maid and a large tea-basket, is trotting leisurely along a white highroad behind a good-natured pony, evidently an old friend of the family.

By and by they leave the road, and with a slower progress, along a cart-track, up gentle uplands—Eastshire is a flat country—reach the scene of Mrs. Bevis' labors.

It is a large field of near sixty acres, and at first he does not see her. He only sees a wide stretch of rural pleasantness—commonplace, and yet delectable—overvaulted by a great faint sky arch, the settled fairness of whose pallid blue is only emphasized by the evidently idle and empty little frivolous cloudlets here and there asleep on its still expanse.

In mid-field is the quickly rising stack, the large area of bared stubble around it evidencing that the barley is half carried. Beside the stack stands an unloading wagon; another, far down the field by the fast-vanishing sheaves, being loaded; two more going and coming, empty and full.

But, as far as he can see, no Mrs. Bevis! Perhaps she has sought the shelter of the stack from the sun, which, though beginning to lower, is still forcible. He shall find her there with book and work, though no expanded parasol hints at her presence. She must be on the farther side.

He approaches the stack, on which the men are singing cheerfully, and chaffing each other as their edifice rises rapidly. He has reached the scaffolding from which the men are pitching. They are too busy to afford him any notice; but a little chubby boy, astride on a cart horse, whose shoulders his short legs fail to reach, stares stolidly at him. Still no Mrs. Bevis.

He was standing irresolute, looking vaguely in the direction of an advancing loaded wain, when in the stalwart female figure at the head of the leader he recognizes something of a likeness to his hostess.

He had never seen Mrs. Bevis in a weather-beaten straw hat, with ears of barley sticking in it, nor heard her calling in tones of Stentor admonishment to a team of cart horses " Peggy ! " " Polly ! " and yet the idea strikes him that it must be she.

We are all, and women especially, mortifyingly dependent for our identity upon our clothes, and he is so little sure of Mrs. Bevis' that he is afraid of seeming to hurry too openly to meet one who may turn out, after all, to be a perfect stranger. His doubts vanish as he nears her, and she stops her team to greet him.

"You *are* energetic!" he says, with a glance of kindly amusement at her sunburnt face and the big cart whip in her hand. "But isn't it rather a severe game in this weather, to play at being your own wagoner?"

"*Play!*" repeats she, with an accent of surprise less disguised than had been that of the pretty parlor maid: "there is not much *play* about it. I always lead every day through the harvest. They"—with a glance at the harvestmen—"would think the world was coming to an end if I did not."

"And am I to 'lead,' too?"

"Not to-day; you may have a holiday to-day. You are much too finely dressed. To-morrow you shall put on your old clothes—I hope you have brought some old clothes—and we will set you to work. You do not mind work, do you?"

But he does not answer. It is not because he could not give a satisfactory response, but because not one of his senses is any longer at the service of the lady who is addressing him. They have all gone out of him for the moment to meet another.

The dialogue is being carried on at a couple of hundred yards from the center of interest, the stack, and the faces of both speakers are turned toward it.

A wagon, which has just finished unloading, is setting off on its light and empty return journey to the sheaves. Beside it walks a female figure—walks, that is, for a step or two beside her horses, and when they are well in motion reaches a hand up to the wagon-tilt, and leaps lightly on to the shaft, thence gracefully swings herself up erect, and stands slight and straight, supporting herself by the tilt. It is obvious that she is perfectly at home and at ease there, for she cracks her whip, and away the heavy horses go in a lumbering trot, that as they pass the stationary wagon breaks into a gallop.

As she passes them the young charioteer flings down a grave smile, and upon that smile it seems to Harry afterward that she had galloped—cart horses, wagon, and all—straight into his heart. He looks, as on after-reflection he concludes he must have done, so overcome and bewildered that his hostess laughs.

"She is wonderfully active, isn't she? I always tell her that she would have made her fortune in a circus."

Then, as his eyes eagerly ask the question which his lips do not frame: "You have never met Honor before? I thought you might in London; not that she is much to be met anywhere. Her name is Honor Lisle, and it is a fixed law that she always comes to help me with the harvest, and sings sentimental songs at the 'frolic' afterward."

"The 'frolic'?"

"Yes; we have a harvest supper. They call it the 'frolic' down here."

He asks no more questions, but his eyes follow the little slender figure holding itself so upright, and yet adapting itself so nicely to the sways and jolts of its uneven course over the stubble. It would be impossible to conceive a more incongruous or absurd idea than that of his mother standing on the tilt of a cart cracking a carter's whip, and yet it is of her that he has been reminded as the odd and lovely vision galloped by.

When he at length turns his gaze away, he finds

that Mrs. Bevis, having chirruped up her Peggy and Polly, has left him to pursue her labors. He hurries compunctiously after her, and finds her, having just exchanged her loaded wagon for an empty one, setting off on her return journey. He walks along beside her, and about mid-field they are again met and crossed by Miss Honor. This time, with a towering load of nodding sheaves behind her, there is no question of galloping. She is sitting tranquilly on the shaft, with her legs dangling. Harry cannot make up his mind which of the two attitudes is the more heavenly graceful and womanly.

All work and no play makes Jack a dull boy; and by and by there is a relaxation of toil, a half hour of recumbent rest, when mistress and men drink their well-earned tea, the men beneath the hedge, the ladies and their guest under the lee of the stack. The guest has been presented to Miss Lisle, and she has looked at him with a large, liquid, mute gaze, and suffered rather than encouraged him to help her in making tea and spreading bread-and-jam—a task which is evidently a daily one to her, and one to which she amply suffices without his aid. It seems to him as if someone had left him a legacy when she asks him—it is the first remark with which she has enriched his ear—whether he minds helping himself to sugar with his fingers. He does not like sugary tea, but he goes on putting lumps into his cup because he feels that she expects it of him.

When, her labors of civility ended, and no one can say that she scamps them, she leans back against the warm barley wall behind her with a little sigh of content, Clarence has placed himself exactly opposite, so that, without offense, he is able to steal frequent looks at her. Even if it were with offense, he would have to do it; and, after all, none can blame a man for the form of filial piety evidenced by staring at a woman because she is like his mother. And she *is* like her: one of those curious accidental likenesses, strong and causeless, which one sometimes meets with, and which lend a piquancy to the contrasts in character which naturally accompany them. Not even the difference in costume from anything he has ever seen his mother wear succeeds in diminishing the likeness. She wears a white sunbonnet, a dark short skirt and white shirt, with a large red and white spotted kerchief crossed over her chest, and at the bottom of the sunbonnet shine gravely two dark antelope eyes, soft yet lucent, that make the strongest feature in the similarity which has struck him.

He has as yet scarcely heard her speak. Will her voice carry on the illusion? It would seem that there would not be much difficulty in finding an observation to make to a lady with whom you are drinking tea in the perfect informality of a stack-shade and a brown glazed teapot; but, after much effort, he can find nothing better than a platitude upon her activity, which he worsens by tacking on to it—lugged in, as he feels, by the head and shoulders, and foolishly applied to her—

"Witching the world with noble horsemanship,"

a line whose unsuitable purple shines like a patch of velvet upon his drugget.

She looks at him from the depths of her dimity tunnel with unaffected surprise and inquiry.

"But surely," she says gravely, "you do not call leading a wagon horsemanship?"

Her voice, too, is like his mother's—at least, it is as low and round; but he is not able to enjoy the discovery, as he is too overcome by the matter-of-fact astonishment with which his lame compliment has been received.

It is clear that nothing is further from the girl's intention than to snub him, and yet it is with a disagreeably small feeling, coupled with a momentary wonder at any educated person not recognizing such a Shakesperian commonplace, that he mutters something about its being a quotation. His *amour propre* is not further soothed by the undisguised mirth with which Mrs. Bevis receives the result of his conversational essay.

"I must advise you not to waste any quotations upon Honor. She never willingly opens a book."

Clarence looks involuntarily at the person accused, expecting a disclaimer as strong as the extreme gentleness of her voice will permit; but none, or any attempt at such, comes. The crime of which she is accused is evidently no crime in her eyes.

"I do not like reading," she acquiesces gravely; adding, as if stating a truism: "I think it is such a waste of time!"

His blue eyes open wide, while Mrs. Bevis goes on laughing:

"Waste of time! Well that *is* a new point of view!"

"Is it? Why, surely,"—speaking with the most perfect frank simplicity, and without the slightest wish to be, or dream of being, thought eccentric,— "surely it is a waste of time to be indoors when you can be out!"

She looks up skyward as she speaks, and half opens her lips with a sigh of pleasure, as if to take in a drink of heaven's good air.

"But in winter—in winter evenings? You cannot be out of doors then?"

"I am always out till long after dark; and when I come in, if I take up a book—— Mrs. Bevis is wrong in saying that I never read; I sometimes have to, when there is nothing better to do, but I almost always fall asleep."

The confession is made without the smallest sign of shame, and remains unremonstrated upon. One of the hearers has heard it often before, while the other——

The harvesters have finished their tea, and their wives have begun anew to ply their rakes, their draggling, bunchy gowns and tawdry-flowered hats making a striking contrast to the short, plain, lovely succinctness of Miss Lisle's costume. But, poor souls! were they Aphrodites dressed by Doucet, where would they be beside her? He sees her afterward dressed in many pretty fashions, but it is in her white sunbonnet that she will go down to his grave with him.

CHAPTER IV.

"Light thickens, and the crow
Makes wing to the rooky wood."

IT seems a pity that the barley should not be finished carrying; so they all work on with a will until the sun has long withdrawn his shining, and his silver sister is holding her scepter over the shorn field. All three jog home together in a little Norfolk cart, but the course taken is a more uneven one than that of the level highroad by which Clarence had been brought; for Miss Honor, who drives, in order to abridge their return journey—since they are indeed late—takes them in a straight line, with hardly more divergences than the proverbial crow. But, since they have a good many more obstacles to encounter than the bird in his sky-meadow, it seems to the stranger several times that they must infallibly upset. But the charioteer evidently knows both the country and the limits of the powers of endurance of her chariot; for though they are several times at an angle which seems to insure instant overthrow,—Mrs. Bevis and Honor towering up skyward on the top of some ridge or ditch-edge, while he himself sinks below the horizon, or *vice versa*,—yet, to the surprise of no one but himself (the ladies have taken their inequalities and peril as the most matter-of-course of daily incidents), they are all landed safely at the stable door. Here, to his surprise, but again as a matter of course to his companions, no groom appearing, Mrs. Bevis and Honor unharness the pony and lead him into his stable.

Mrs. Bevis' house is undoubtedly a cottage whose thick walls, small-paned windows, and window-seats tell its ripe age; but it has none of a cottage's squeeziness. A put-out wing here, expanded offices there, give it ease and commodity. A long narrow drawing room, born of the knocking two smaller rooms into one, runs along the garden front, with its light tempered by a creeper-smothered veranda where William Allen Richardson slips his oranged blossoms through a tangle of jessamine, and where a luxuriant vine has to be pushed away from the casement windows above, like hair out of a maid's eyes, to enable one to see out.

Clarence makes these and other discoveries next morning, when, having risen early, he passes through the already air and sun sweetened house to the square flower garden beyond—the square garden cunningly sunk between sloped grass-banks to protect it from the keenness of the Eastshire winds. It is now gorgeous with a dewy crowd of late summer jewels—gaillardia and chrysanthemums, gladioli and dahlias. He had thought to have had these morning pleasantnesses to himself, or shared them only with the gardener scything the terrace banks; but he has not made three steps on its sward before he perceives Miss Lisle standing by a green tub—one of several that adorn the parterre—overbrimming with flowering geraniums, and with a hanging fringe of sweet peas fragrantly depending from it. She has a green-and-red parrot on her shoulder, and another on her finger.

He had been surprised as he came through the house to hear the crying of an infant, and now discovers that the sound proceeds from one of the parrots, who is giving a very lifelike rendering of the squalls of an extremely angry baby, greatly aided therein by Miss Honor herself, who assists his memory with her own voice.

She is so occupied that she does not perceive him till he is close upon her; nor does it strike him that she is particularly pleased when she does. She stops squalling, though the bird continues, and her face stiffens—unnecessarily, as he thinks.

"How well he does it! How well you have taught him!"

"I did not teach him. They have just arrived from Venezuela; and I suppose they heard the black babies crying there."

Her voice is sweet and civil, but her manner is prim. It is clear that she does not want him. The conviction makes him feel awkward.

"At least you help him not to forget his accomplishment?"

"I can always talk to birds."

The statement is a simple one, yet it seems to convey an implication that she neither is nor desires to be as conversationally successful with her own kind. He wishes vaguely that he could gracefully leave her. She saves him the trouble, moving softly houseward in her coarse blue serge gown, with a red-and-yellow bandanna knotted loosely round her pretty brown throat, and with the black baby's counterfeit still persistently yammering in his green-and-red on her shoulder.

"You have been making friends with Honor, over her parrots?"

It is the cordial voice of his hostess, crossing the sward to meet him.

"H'm!"—doubtfully—"I am afraid the friendliness was rather lopsided. Why is she so very stand-off?"

Mrs. Bevis shrugs her shoulders.

"I am afraid her first impulse on meeting a stranger—a strange man, that is—is to put all her bristles up. They are not very formidable ones,"—smiling,—"and if you knew the kind of men with whom she is habitually thrown—if you knew her story, in fact, you would not wonder."

Certainly Clarence asks nothing better than to know it. They have stepped up and off the little grass bank to the terrace walk above it, whose low close ivy hedge, topping a haha, divides it from the field, where an old chestnut mare is cropping the grass. Clarence wishes that she was not, since her owner stops to wish her a kind good-morning before going on:

"You know that her father is Algernon Lisle, the well-known racing man?"

"I did not know it."

"But you have heard of him?"

"Naturally!" with emphasis.

"You know the sort of character he bears—the sort of company he keeps?"

"And"—precipitately—"has she to keep it, too?" Mrs. Bevis gives a rather melancholy nod.

"To a certain extent, yes. Isn't it disgraceful? But, happily, what she has most to suffer from is neglect. He leaves her alone for months together at a large, dreary, half-dismantled place he has in the country; and it is only now and then that he swoops down upon her with a horde of doubtful ladies and shady sporting men, most of whom, as far as I can make out, persecute her with extremely equivocal attentions."

"And does she class me with them?" in a wounded voice.

"Oh, no, no! But she has got, poor child! into a habit of self-defense; and, really, deplorable as the situation is, it—such companionship, I mean—does her less harm than it would to anyone else in the world. She has the most extraordinary faculty of shaking water off her feathers."

He does not interrupt her by a word, but there is such a look of mingled indignation and interest in his look that she gives him an approving glance and goes on :

"She is not in the least innocent, in the mistaken sense in which that word is generally employed as a synonym for 'ignorant.' How should she be, with her upbringing? No, Honor is the least ignorant of evil, and the most really innocent girl I have ever met. Do you understand?"

Thus directly stated, it would be odd if he did not; and even if the possibility of the combination suggested were at first difficult of belief to him, a week in the company of her of whom it is predicated renders it a dogma from which neither torture nor death could sever him.

That week—that wonderful week! Its days mounting in stages from the "good" of the first sight of her in triumphant gallop on her wagon-tilt, through the "better" of the subsequent talks through the half hour of rest for tea under the waxing stack on later days, to the "best" of the final day's shrimping.

Her slight frost has thawed under the careful reverence of his manner, and as early as the second evening he has made successful breaches in her taciturnity. She is never a great talker, but she lets him, by and by, have glimpses into her life. He would not have understood them if he had not had Mrs. Bevis' previous hints to enlighten him, as Honor never makes the smallest complaint of her lot; but they sufficiently conform to his hostess' account of the girl's mode of existence to fill up the measure of his tender pity.

By the week end he is in a trance of ecstasy over her odd duodecimo beauty, her strange accomplishments, her pretty pluck, her silences, her snatches of short speech. And yet he is a bookish man, and she never for one moment blenches or wavers in her strong and consistent assertion of her detestation of all book-learning.

"Does she really hate reading?" he asks Mrs. Bevis, as they sit smoking cigarettes opposite each other, sunk in deep wicker armchairs in the red-papered, white-dadoed sitting hall.

"If she says so"—laughing—"you may be sure that she does, for she is the most absolutely looking-glassly truthful person I ever met. Yes, really and truly, she does hate the sight of a book. I want to try to reconcile her a little to them. I shall never do much"—laughing again—"but you will help me?"

"I shall be delighted; but how?"

"We do not go to the harvest field till after luncheon to-morrow; you might pick out something short and attractive to read to us in the morning out-of-doors."

"Prose or verse?"

"Not verse, certainly. She is of Hotspur's opinion, and would 'rather hear a dry wheel grate on the axle-tree.'"

"Incredible! With that face!"

"But she knows a good deal, too, of an out-of-the-way sort. Her knowledge of birds and beasts and their ways puts me, and would, I dare say, put you, too, to shame."

"It might easily do that."

The proposed morning's reading to improve Honor's mind never comes off, so many outdoor temptations arise to prevent it; but on Sunday evening, as they sit in the library, the dropped subject is taken up.

Of all the rooms in the exquisitely comfortable cottage-house, the library is Clarence's favorite. The library was once a kitchen, whose wide-yawning chimney, though now decorated by a high, white, carved-wood chimney-piece, and surmounted by a white-framed mirror, betrays by its hospitable bigness its original intention.

The evening, though August, is chilly, and a driftwood fire flickers on the bookshelves that almost hide the walls, laden with inviting and obviously readable books, wooing the student's hand to take them from under their red leather flap. The walls are red, too, wherever the books allow them to show their genial face, and white Portugal china pleasantly tops the shelves. A better setting for a literary treat could not be imagined. Honor has placed herself on a straight-backed chair, so as to be less susceptible of the allurements of slumber. Mrs. Bevis lies back in her sofa corner, with the enjoyment of rest of a habitually active woman after a week's harvesting.

Clarence, having carefully chosen his book, "The Outcasts of Poker Flat," begins. It impossible that anyone short of the Seven Sleepers, or Mr. Wardle's *Joe*, could fall asleep over Bret Harte.

It has always been one of the choicest pleasures of his mother's life to be read aloud to by him, and from other lips besides her fondly prejudiced ones he has received compliments upon his reading. His mother has always worked while he read, though often in the ardor of listening the dainty crewel or cambric has dropped from her fingers into her lap. Honor never works, and he shrewdly suspects her of not possessing the necessary implements— scissors, thread, or thimble. She sits straight up now, with her eyes fixed upon him. At first it makes him nervous, and he has an inclination to ask her to look away. But presently the consciousness that those worlds of pensive fire are upon him spirits him up to a more sympathetic rendering of his author. He is

conscious of having never before read so well. This
feeling is heightened when she presently alters her
position, and, still gazing fixedly at him, leans her
arms upon the table before her, as if to bring sight
and hearing closer to the focus of interest. He steals
a glance at her as he nears the climax. A film—is it
of gathering tears?—is stealing over the large dark
pupils; and as the infinitely pathetic catastrophe is
reached, the little lovely head falls forward on the
outstretched arms.

He has triumphed. She will not let him see her
tears, but she will never again say that she hates
books. But will she not?

"Isn't it incredible that even that could not keep
her awake?" asks Mrs. Bevis, in a voice still strangled
by her own emotion at the well-known yet ever-wondrous story. "Honor, I am ashamed of you!"

At the vigorous shoulder-shake which accompanies
this expression of opinion, the girl stirs, lifts her head,
and opens two eyes, dry as bones, but heavy with
unmistakable slumber. As they light on Clarence,
the dreamy look gives way to one of sincere contrition.

"I am so sorry," she says quietly, "but I told you
how it would be. I *did* try to keep awake, and for a
time I thought I had succeeded; but then your voice
went on and on" (he had imagined that he had varied
its tones so subtly), "and it was too much for me.
But I beg your pardon."

. . . . .

This mortification—and it is at first an acute one—
is the sole blot on that kingly week. Even it turns

out to be a blessing in disguise, Honor's compunction for the wound she has inflicted drawing her more out of her shell than had any of his efforts to conciliate her. She has not expressed her repentance in words, of which she has never a very large store, but by little graciousnesses and a general drawing nearer to him than before the catastrophe. By the time that the shrimping day is reached, that supreme last day, he is actually glad that she had fallen asleep over his reading.

By the shrimping day the harvest is all in. Mrs. Bevis would not otherwise have countenanced, much less shared, such a faithless frivolity. The harvest is in, and the "frolic" that crowns it over. The frolic takes place in the great barn. Mrs. Bevis has opened the ball with the "Lord of the Harvest," and Miss Lisle has danced down all her fellow-toilers and returned thanks at supper for her own health, drunk with clamorous applause, in a succinct little speech delivered without hesitation and with not a superfluous word. And now it is the succeeding afternoon, and the three friends are driving down in the Norfolk cart to the sands. Honor drives, up and down, over the sand-hills, serenely indifferent to jolts and lurches. A basket of provisions, shrimping-nets, etc., has been carefully put in by her. She and her hostess are wrapped to their heels in long blue cloaks with red hoods. Arrived, they unpack the cart, and tether the pony among the sparse sea-grass and sea-hollies.

Clarence has turned away for a moment to scan the sea—rather rough to-day—and, on looking back, gives a start.

Honor is stripped of her cloak and hat, and stands in her shrimping-costume before him—bare legs and feet, a blue serge blouse belted round her slender waist, and with a square red sailor collar and blue knickerbockers. A red silk handkerchief is tied over her sleek black head.

She stands with perfect *sangfroid*, getting ready her net. He could not have believed that bare legs and knickerbockers could be consistent with so dignified a composure. He fears, the moment after he has uttered it, that it is not in perfect taste, but the ejaculation seems forced from him :

"What a very pretty dress !"

"Most people like it," replied she, calmly acquiescent in his admiration as nothing odd or novel—"everybody, I think, except my nurse, Mrs. Nasmyth ; she cannot bear to see me in it ; she would like to burn it."

"She cannot be a person of much perception, your nurse, Mrs.——"

He hesitates at the unusual name, and she supplies it :

"Nasmyth."

"Nasmyth," repeats he, putting his hand to his forehead, while a faint ripple of recollection runs over his memory. "In the dark ages, many, many years ago, I, too, had a nurse of that name. Do you think that she can by any possibility be the same person ?"

"If she were, I should think that she would have mentioned you."

"If she were," returns he, oddly stirred by the

idea, "it would constitute a sort of relationship between us—like being god-children of the same person."

She does not answer, except by a look, which has once or twice before puzzled him—very full and direct, and yet with a half frown, as if not fully comprehending, or else not liking to accept, his drift.

He is not sure that he has not displeased her. But if he has, it is a very passing shadow.

It is in perfect amity that all walk over the sands together. The two ladies have entered the frothy sea, and it is with a penetrating sense of annoyance that the young man sees Honor going deeper and deeper into the heaving waves. He feels profoundly chagrined at being prevented by the unsuitability of his dress from following her.

Pushing her net before her, she goes, stirring up the sand in which the shrimps are found, and ever and anon pulling it up to see what luck she has had.

He walks along the dry shore parallel and tantalized, shouting remarks to her, of which the singing sea-wind carries away half; and she sending him back little words across the intervening fringe of breakers, telling him that on bad days she has to go in deeper than on fair ones, and that she had been in up to her neck before now.

After a while she emerges, dripping, and radiant with success. The hostess follows. Both re-envelop themselves in their blue cloaks, and, making a fire—in this, at least, he can help—put on a little pot brought with them, and cook the shrimps in it. They are inclosed in a small net-bag; a great lump of extra salt is put into the sea-water in which they are boiled, and when, after three or four minutes, the transparent bodies have turned solid, the water is poured off, and everyone, putting in his finger and thumb, helps himself.

Honor has, as on the harvest day, cut bread and butter. The shrimps are piping hot, and was there ever such a princely banquet?

They are quite sheltered from the land breezes by a protecting sand-hill, and after the feast is ended the two fisherwomen race along the beach to dry themselves. He runs, too, for company.

It is growing toward sunsetting, and the path of gold that leads straight to the sun moves with them on the wet sand as they run. Long pinkish tongues of sand that run out into the sea are getting uncovered by the ebbing tide.

Then they pack up, and bump home again in the cart.

"We shall not let you be a looker-on next time," says the hostess. "Next time you must come more suitably appareled."

His eye brightens.

"Then there is to be a next time?"

"I should rather think so!" with great cordiality.

"It will not be my fault if——" he begins, with a headlong impulse of acceptance, then breaks off short.

Once again, in the low red light, he feels the great stag-eyes opposite looking doubtfully at him out of the beloved little face, which has been kissed into brighter beauty by the pungent sea air.

· · · · ·

The last sight he has of her next morning is standing at the wicket gate, with one green-and-red parrot on her shoulder and the other on her finger, as he had found her on the dewy grass plot. But her face is no longer prim. He is almost quite sure that she is sorry he is going.

CHAPTER V.

THE Linleys' child—the one that is not quite right in the head—must be ill, for it has not been out in its perambulator for two days, and now the others are going out without it.

This interesting piece of news has been given to Mrs. Clarence by her cousin, Abigail Dent, who, standing as she does a great part of the day at the drawing-room window, is in a position to keep her hostess posted in every detail that can be gleaned from their exits and entrances, their tradesmen's carts, their maids' flirting capped heads down the areas, and their own occasional appearances at their windows pulling up or letting down blinds, of her neighbors' lives.

During the week of Abigail's visit (she arrived on the day of Harry's departure, and he has been gone—a slight sigh escapes his mother as she makes the reflection—a whole week) Mrs. Clarence has learned more of the history, habits, and character of her neighbors than an æon of her own unassisted observation would have taught her. To most people the deadest street in dead St. Gratian would not seem to afford much matter for close and acutely interested study, but to Abigail, fresh from the yet deader depths of a parish in the Lincolnshire Fens, it seems a second Piccadilly.

Nor is she niggard of the information reaped—over-bounteous rather, though that she thinks so no one would guess from the listener's manner. The remark about the afflicted little Linley calls forth only the patient and rather apologetic rejoinder:

"I am afraid I do not quite remember who the Linleys are."

"They are the doctor's family. He ought to have his night-bell mended; it is broken. There was a man pulling at it for half an hour last night."

"Was there, indeed?"

That our words and thoughts do often not very closely tally is a truism of truisms, and no one who heard this languid query would divine the far from languid aspiration that accompanies it—an aspiration to dislodge Abigail from her post at the window—that post of observation upon Harry's return which has always been his mother's, and which this girl is in all innocence usurping.

It needs but a word, and the child would eagerly yield it; but the fear that is always with Mrs. Clarence, of making her son ridiculous through overshow of affection, restrains her, and the word remains unspoken, while she sits on in her prospectless armchair, and receives with outward sweetness such further scraps of information as Miss Abigail chooses to throw her.

For some time they are of a not more agitating type than that, from his manner of running down the street with his tail lowered, she is sure that the Hicksons' dog is out without leave, and that the Jameses' housemaid is cleaning the top windows, sitting on the ledge outside, with the window shut down upon her knees, and "Isn't it very dangerous?" But when these announcements are exchanged for a series of ejaculations : " This must be Harry ! There is an H. C. on the portmanteau. It *is* Harry ! How well he looks—burnt as brown as a berry ! I will run down and let him in ! "—when this point is reached, and the girl runs toward the door, strained nature gives way, and with " No, no, dear ; please not : I always let him in myself," Mrs. Clarence puts her young cousin gently aside, and passes out and down so swiftly that she has reached and opened the door as he drives up. She draws a long breath of relief as she does so. It would have been a bad omen if she had been just too late, and she would not have liked a bad omen to-day, of all days, though she could not have told you why.

He is too busy at first paying his cab, with his back turned to her, for her to get a good view of his face. When she does, she is aware of an unqualifiable change in it. She tries to tell herself that it is only the effect of that sun and sea-wind tan which Abigail has described as " burnt as brown as a berry," but she knows in her own heart that it is something different. He kisses her with what she knows he means to be his usual eager tenderness ; but to her it seems that his kiss is scamped, and curtailed by his breaking off to greet his little cousin, whose seventeen-year-old fortitude has broken down to the extent of letting her appear at the stairtop, peeping rosily over the banisters.

Nor, when they are in the drawing room, does he

show any comfortable inclination to sit down at her feet and tell her all about it, as on his return from circuit, or, indeed, from any former absences. He walks about restlessly; compliments Abigail on her growth, for which, as his mother feels, he yet has no real eyes; moves a chair out of its place; kicks aside a footstool, and at last ejaculates, in an oppressed voice:

"How close your room feels! Are the windows open? But there never is any ozone in this air. Ozone is one of the things that this dear little town is chronically out of."

He laughs, but with such an accent of disgust that his mother steals a look of surprised inquiry at him as she says:

"I am afraid we must confess that in the matter of breezes we do not compare favorably with the Broads."

"I was not near the Broads."

"No?"

Faithful to her lifelong rule, she adds no question, and at first he seems disinclined to go further in correcting the mistake in her supposition. He takes another fidgety stroll round, and then says, half apologetically:

"I suppose it is the entirely outdoor life which I have been leading that makes me feel any house stuffy."

She takes this crumb of incidental information gratefully.

"You have been a great deal out of doors? I thought you would. I was glad of the fine weather for you."

"And you—you and Abigail? How have you been getting on?"

If Mrs. Clarence is disappointed at this diversion of the stream into another channel, just as she had hoped that it had begun to flow toward her, she shows no sign.

"We have been waiting to 'get on' till you came back to give us a push. We have been standing still, haven't we, Abigail?"

"It has been *delightful!*" replies Abigail, with an accent of heartfelt sincerity. "Oh, if Lord Rosebery would but give father a *town* living! How can anyone that can help it live in the country?"

"'*How can anyone that can help it live in the country!*'" repeats Harry, in a tone of such mixed stupefaction, and yet absence, that his mother gives a slight puzzled laugh.

"You do not indorse that sentiment? You have been finding country pleasures less contemptible than Abigail does?"

So vague and neutral an inquiry can scarcely be held an infringement of her rule, and it gets no answer but an unadorned "Yes."

"You have enjoyed yourself?"

"Yes."

The second "Yes" is as unadorned as the first, and has no intentional emphasis about it; but yet to his mother's ear, love-practiced in his tones, it conveys an idea of acuter enjoyment than had it been escorted by half a dozen ecstatic adjectives.

It is not till much later in the evening—not till Abigail has regretfully gone to bed, after offering her cousin many innocent and Miranda-like attentions, which rather embarrass him—that Mrs. Clarence gets any more light upon her son's visit; and even then the facts communicated seem inadequate to account for the thrill of that "Yes," which still echoes in her frightened ears.

The conversation begins indifferently.

"She is a dear little thing, isn't she?" asks Mrs. Clarence, as the door shuts upon the young visitor, and with an astute caution in not rushing too immediately upon the topic she is longing to approach.

He starts.

"A dear little thing! Who is a dear little thing?"

"Why, Abigail."

"Abigail! Of course! Yes, a dear little thing, and," with an obvious effort to pull himself together and attend, "and so much grown, too!"

"But do not let us talk about Abigail."

"No?"

"Let us talk about *you*."

"Is that a much more interesting theme?"

"Well, to me it is."

He drops a light kiss on the top of her head as an acknowledgment of this expression of interest, and sits down for the first time since his arrival on a stool at her feet. But he keeps his face half averted from her as he leans against her knees, and though it is an attitude that he has often previously taken, she cannot help a suspicion that it is now chosen intentionally.

And yet what is there in the facts which he rather slowly communicates in the course of the next hour that would seem to call for disguise? That he has been very much both impressed and possessed by his hostess' mode of life, at once patriarchal and intellectual, is patent. But though he speaks with bated breath both of the flavor of her cigarettes, imported direct from Turkey, and of the half-finished essay she has shown him upon the analogies between the teaching of Plato and Browning, yet the tone of his outspoken admiration, reassuringly direct and straightforward, sufficiently convinces his listener that it is not Mrs. Bevis herself with whom the danger so faintly, yet surely scented, lies. With whom, then? No hint has escaped the narrator of any other possible source, not even when a subtly framed query might naturally have surprised an unintended admission.

"And you did not get tired of your *tête-à-tête* in a whole week?"

An almost imperceptible pause.

"It can hardly be called a *tête-à-tête* when you are chaperoned by a whole field of harvesters; and, besides, a friend of Mrs. Bevis' who knows a good deal about farming, and who always helps her with her harvest, was there."

"A neighboring squire, I suppose?"

"No-o; staying in the house."

The downward slope is insidiously gradual. At the beginning of the conversation no idea of concealing the sex of his co-guest from his mother had occurred to Clarence. But, now that she herself has fallen into the error of concluding that a "friend who knows a good deal about farming" must necessarily be a man, why should he hinder her from continuing in it? It is she who has deceived herself, not he her; and through her mistake he sees a way of escaping from an *impasse* out of which he has hitherto discerned no likely issue.

Despite her lifelong efforts to hide them, he is as well aware as she of the jealous terrors that always devour her when she knows that he is in the company of young and attractive women. Up to the present time he has often taken a teasing pleasure in heightening her empty alarms, secure, in the clearness of heart and conscience, of being able to dissipate them by a word. This time he has been tormented by the problem how to baffle the anxious penetration of her loving eyes while describing, in however chastened a style, the woman who had galloped into his burnt heart on a wagon-tilt. But if his mother takes it for granted that the agriculturist alluded to was a man, the difficulty is not only evaded, but escaped. Her curiosity will be but slightly aroused, and he may tell her just as much or as little as he pleases. The result shows the accuracy of his calculations.

"You must have been a nice, harmonious little party," she says, with contented-looking approbation. "I do not wonder that with such surroundings and such a cook"—smiling—"with your sailings, and shrimpings, and harvestings, you enjoyed yourself. I am *so* glad that you made Mrs. Bevis' acquaintance. She is a friend after my own heart for you. I hope you will often go there again; are you invited?"

"Oh, yes, I have a general invitation."

She looks so relieved and so softly beaming with

joy at having once again regained her treasure unimpaired, that his heart smites him.

"But you know general invitations do not count for much," he says, with a dim feeling that he must make amends to her for his duplicity. "Out of sight, out of mind, you know."

He has resumed his uneasy patrol, and when she goes to bed, she leaves him still at it.

. . . . .

The Bramshill family are strown about the ground under the beeches, which give their name to the domain, like skittles at the end of a game. The heat has been the means of thus disposing them, even their force of mind and body succumbing to the weather. The judge indeed, who feels and grumbles at the heat a good deal more than if he had passed his life in Greenland, is sitting in his darkened study bewailing his lost punkah; but his wife and such of his sons as are not pursuing their professions in foreign lands, or have been unsuccessful in securing invitations to the moors, and his one fair daughter, are all arranged in different crawling, kicking, lounging, dozing attitudes on the parched grass at the only spot in the grounds where a breeze sent by the near-sliding river is faintly felt. The one drawback to this delectable summer spot is that it lies in full view of the carriage drive, at the mercy of every arriving vehicle, making the "not at home," so dear and familiar to most mouths, a dead letter.

Euphemia lies in a hammock, slowly swinging an immense length of white crêpon, sending the hot but always obedient youths on many trifling and not-very necessary errands, and frequently refreshing herself with libations from a jug of iced coffee at her elbow. Occasionally she flings down among her subjects scraps of information out of a journal she is turning over. Most of her family are reading to themselves, and in such cases it is tiresome to have fragments of another person's literature forced upon you, but not a murmur is raised.

"There were forty-five thousand visitors at Constantinople on Bank Holiday."

The nearest brother, who has been lying on his back, rolls over on his face, but nothing occurs to him to say.

"Forty-five thousand! it makes one gasp to think of it," comments Lady Bramshill.

"I do not know how many visitors there may have been at Constantinople on Bank Holiday, but I'm blessed if there are not visitors to The Beeches to-day. Do not you hear wheels?" asks another brother, sitting up and cocking an anxious ear.

In a second they are all erect in distrustful sitting postures, and in another second, the eye having confirmed the evidence of the ear, they have all sprung to their feet and scudded away, swift as the evening rabbit.

"There they go, silly fellows!" ejaculates their mother, with a lenient sigh. "You will not go, too, will you, Euphemia?"

"Nothing is further from my thoughts," replies the young lady composedly, still swinging and sipping. "If they are anybody pleasant—I cannot imagine anything less likely—you might bring them out to me."

Lady Bramshill makes such haste to comply as the hoisting herself out of a deep beehive chair will admit; but before she has made three steps across the sward, she sees the unwelcome company, led by the butler, advancing straight to the family's cool beechen lair. To Lady Bramshill herself, being one to whom society of no sort comes amiss, they are not unwelcome, even before she recognizes in the slender, smoke-color-clad figure, who is a little in front of two unknown ones, her girlhood's hitherto not very expansive friend.

"Better late than never!" cried she heartily. "What do you mean by letting a whole week pass without ever coming near us? But we will not begin to quarrel at once. And so this is *little* Harry!" looking at him with kindly stupefaction, and holding out her left hand to him, since her right still clasps his mother's. "Ah, Mr. Harry! so it was you whom I saw in the post office. *Little* Harry indeed! Ha, ha! I must present you to *little* Euphemia. Euphemia, come and be presented to my dear old chum, Lucy Clarence, and make acquaintance with that extreme rarity, a man who is taller than you—ha, ha! Euphemia's one search in life"—laughing proudly—"is to find a man whom she is not obliged to look down upon."

Euphemia, in answer to this eager appeal, has swung herself with protesting slowness out of her hammock—such slowness that by the time she stands erect beside it the visitors have reached the beechen shade. She pays the proper civilities prettily enough to Mrs. Clarence, though her own parent is by no means sure that there is not a lurking displeasure in the tail of her eye, and then critically surveys, with eyes about on a level with his own, the young man.

"I hope," she says calmly, "that you will join me in resistance, if my mother insists upon measuring us together. Much of my life is spent in protesting against having to stand back-to-back with every tall man I meet on first introduction."

He has no instant answer, surprised at her tone; the youthfulness of her appearance, coupled with the cool *aplomb* of her address, impressing him disagreeably.

"I do really believe that she is the taller of the two, now that they stand together," says Lady Bramshill, with a slight chuckle. "If all trades fail, Lucy, we shall really be able to furnish out a traveling caravan with our own two families—Harry and Euphemia the giants, I the fat woman, the judge——", Her imagination fails to provide the judge with a suitable function in her proposed enterprise, and she runs into another subject: "But I am not going to let you off so easily about your never having been near us all this while. You cannot plead preengagement. Nobody ever has an engagement, pre or not pre, in St. Gratian. There is never anything to do except go to church,—those perpetual church bells would drive *me* cracked,—and even you can't have been in church *all* day."

"I waited till I could bring Harry," replies Mrs. Clarence, with a slight glance, in which the pride, though a good deal more covert than the other mother's, is to the full as deep, at her son; "and he has been away in Eastshire."

"But you might have come first without him, and then with him."

This is undeniable, and the visitor, never very glib in polite inventions, is nonplused.

The conversation, such as it is, has so far lain wholly with the elders; the younger now take it up.

Upon her mother's assertion of her superior stature, Euphemia has subsided again hastily into her hammock, as if resolved to avoid any putting it to the proof, and reclines there with a silent indifference to his presence which the young man is not slow to characterize to himself as "bad form."

The mention of Eastshire seems to give a slight fillip to her attention.

"You have been in Eastshire?" she says.

"Yes."

"In what part?"

The idea—a captious one—occurs to him that the part of the county visited by him is no concern of hers, but he answers:

"Near Norton Regis."

"Near Norton Regis?" repeats she. "Then it must be the same neighborhood. Did you happen to hear of a little place called Briarly Cottage?"

"I not only heard of it, but it was there that I was staying."

"You do not say so!" cries Euphemia, with a great accession of liveliness in her tone. "With Mrs. Bevis—Honor Lisle's Mrs. Bevis? How often I have heard of Mrs. Bevis, and of the joys and glories of Briarly Cottage! And was Honor there? She stays there so much."

"Yes, she was there."

Involuntarily he lowers his voice a little, and his blue eye shoots an apprehensive beam toward his mother. It is possible that no harm is yet done, as the elder pair have, within the last moment or two, drawn something further off, since Lady Bramshill has officiously insisted on her friend's transferring herself from the chair on which she had been sitting in quiet, cool grace to another, pronounced to be a more comfortable one.

In the little bustle consequent on this move Mrs. Clarence may very likely not have heard. She gives no sign of having done so. But this prop is soon knocked from under him.

"Do you hear, mother? Mr. Clarence has been staying in the house with Honor Lisle! Oh, mother, dear!"—in a tone of not very patient remonstrance—"why will not you let people enjoy themselves in their own way? Mrs. Clarence liked the other chair best, or she would not have chosen it."

"I was afraid of the legs. You know it came down with Adolphus yesterday," replies Lady Bramshill mildly; and her daughter goes on:

"Isn't it a curious coincidence that Mr. Clarence should have been staying in the house with Honor Lisle? You do not see the coincidence? Why, Honor Lisle is the odd girl who was at school with me, about whom I have so often talked to you."

The murder is out now; the name and the fact have both been pronounced with an unmistakable bell-clearness, and he sees their instantaneous effect in a to all but him invisible start, and a slight, but hurt and frightened, flush hardly perceptibly staining his mother's cheek.

"The world is ridiculously small," replies Lady Bramshill, with that trite formula which so many of us, who ought to know better, habitually employ. "We never go anywhere that we do not knock up against someone whom we knew in India." Then, since her friend does not take up this brilliant generalization, she goes on: "I dare say you are wondering how we could have sent our only girl to school,—my father had a horror of girls' schools,—but, you see, it could not be helped. We had to keep her here. She was with us in Bengal for only our last year. Really, considering what perfect strangers we were when we met, it is a wonder that we get on as well as we do."

She ends with a laugh of such perfect satisfaction as shows how little *she* sees to condemn in her daughter's manners.

CHAPTER VI.

THE murder is out; and that it should be so through the agency of the long white impertinence in the hammock does not increase Clarence's fondness for her. But it must be confessed that it heightens his interest in her. He has also apparently very greatly heightened her interest in him.

"Do tell me about Honor," she says, in a key of such unfeigned animation as warms his heart to her for a second, only to be cooled to freezing point the next, when to her question she adds, with thoughtful slanginess: "She was about as mad as they make 'em."

Lives there a man with soul so dead as to be able to hear that the object of his heart's high worship is "as mad as they make 'em" without wincing? If there be, Clarence is not he.

"*As mad as they make 'em!*" repeats he, reddening, as he feels, with displeasure at the expression.

"I do not mean that there was the least bit of harm in her," rejoins Euphemia, noting, with some inward amusement, the effect produced by her words, and proceeding, but without haste, to correct the impression made. "She was an innocent sort of creature; but she *was* mad—at least, she was like a very nice sort of savage."

"I think"—with excessive dryness—"that we cannot be speaking of the same person."

"Oh, yes, we are! There are not two Honor Lisles who go to stay with *two* Mrs. Bevises, and who break in horses for them."

"The lady whom I met broke in no horses."

"No, of course, she would not have time at this season of the year, because they must be busy with the harvest. Honor used always to go to Mrs. Bevis for corn harvest. They seem to get it in themselves. It sounds so primeval! I wish they would invite me."

Once again Clarence turns a quick look of distress and new apprehension toward his mother, with a painful recollection of her misunderstanding of his statement as to Mrs. Bevis' assistant harvester, and of his own relieved acquiescence in her remaining in error. That this should be the mode of her enlightenment—a mode of all others most calculated to excite her fears and give her a hurt sense of his duplicity—annoys him inexpressibly. He cannot see her face, as it is turned toward Lady Bramshill, one of whose well-meant attempts to upset the scheme of her neighbors' lives and alter their details she is at the moment engaged in baffling. The effort, in this case, is directed toward making Mrs. Clarence abandon all her tradesmen. The chief battery is directed against the butcher, whose birthright and blessing she is with ardor laboring to take away, and supplant him by a *protégé* of her own.

"He sent me his list,—prices literally wholesale,—so I went to him at once, and have never left him; the best joints exactly half what they charge here—what, I have no doubt, Joddrell is charging you; and though his shop is at Smithfield, he executes, carriage free, any order exceeding five pounds. It would be quite worth your while to go to him. Do not you think so? Do not you think that being able to get rid of the middleman is worth *anything?*"

"Oh, yes, worth anything!" faintly; and her son knows that she has heard.

"I am afraid the young lady is having a very dull time!" says Lady Bramshill, disappointed at the want of enthusiasm manifested by her contemporary, and turning the hose of her officious benevolence on a fresh object. "I am afraid that I did not quite catch your name, my dear Miss—Dent? Oh, thanks! Stupid of me! Now, what can we do for you? Quite happy as you are? Oh, but it is so dull for you! Now, if the boys were here! Where are those boys? Ah, there is Adolphus!—at least, he must be near, because here is Nipper," as a wire-haired terrier squeezes himself through some rhododendrons, expressly to tell the visitors, in volleyed barks, that he "has no use for them." "You may be quite sure if you see one that the other is not far off. Doll, Doll!"

There is a stirring among the bushes, but no further sign of compliance. It is but too apparent that Adolphus is making off in an opposite direction. It will require a stronger spell than his parent's to raise him. That stronger spell is not long wanting.

"Doll!" cries a commanding young voice from the hammock, "why do not you come when you are called? Come here this moment!"

The order needs not to be twice uttered. In immediate obedience to it the branches part and disclose the skulking youth, who now advances with less shame than his too evident effort to avoid them ought to have produced, and is presented to the company, from among whom he presently leads off the delighted Abigail kitchen-garden and plumward.

Clarence looks longingly after them, with no plum hunger indeed, but with an ardent desire to get out of earshot of his mother. Euphemia, however, is otherwise minded.

"I think we will not follow their example," she says luxuriously; "they are young and foolish, and do not know when they are well off. But do tell me more about Honor. Is she as eccentric as she used to be?"

"It depends"—cavilingly—"upon what you call eccentric."

"I think"—laughing—"that there is not a possible definition of the word that would not include her."

He is too much annoyed to ask for an explanation, earnestly as he desires one; but, happily for him, Miss Bramshill needs no urging to enlarge upon the theme.

"She was, as I say, like a very nice savage. She could not bear being indoors, and would far rather have slept under a hedge or a haystack than in bed. She liked all sorts of little wild beasts and birds far better than people, and she never voluntarily opened a book."

The picture, overcharged as it now is, has still enough features of resemblance to the original, as he knows her, to give such liveliness of interest to his listening that the narrator goes on:

"She never could learn anything—or, rather, I suppose, she never *would*. During the whole two years I knew her she was always more or less in disgrace—generally more. But really, poor soul! considering the bad race she comes of, and the execrable surroundings she had always had at home, I think that there was wonderfully little harm in her."

Again Harry is acutely conscious that he is not the only listener. To his chafed sense it seems that the pauses in the talk of the two elder ladies always malevolently coincides with the narration by Euphemia of some fact that he would specially wish his mother not to hear. Is it his fancy that it is only by an effort she is keeping up her gentle answers to, and mild parrying of, Lady Bramshill's fervidly friendly endeavors to induce her to upset her whole scheme of life and remodel it on a new pattern?

"It is such a sinful waste!" she is saying warmly. "You are so fitted to shine. I will ask the judge if it is not so; and I know no one whose opinion, when it is not warped by his prejudices, is better worth having. I am sure that on this question I shall have him upon my side."

"Will you?" very absently.

"If you take the house I mention,—of course, it is not quite up to your requirements yet, but the judge would be only too glad to build on to it for the sake of securing you as neighbors,—we should be even nearer each other than we were at poor old Green Leigh, and you would have the benefit of whatever society we see; and I must say there is generally a dribble of people of one sort or another through the house. And we mean to have Saturdays to Mondays as a regular thing."

This is not a question, so the *distraite* supposed listener, whose listening to another dialogue is not supposed, apparently thinks no answer is required, for she gives none, and her silence quells for a minute or two her friend's loquacity.

It is in this interval that Euphemia resumes:

"Honor must be nineteen now. She is a year older than I am. Has she turned out a beauty? They used to laugh at me, but I always thought it was upon the cards that she would. She had such undeniable 'points.' Has she grown up pretty?"

There is a tiny pause, the hum of the happy little winged peoples that occupy the summer air seeming to emphasize, to his ears, the eagerly attentive silence of one of the human listeners.

"I do not think I am much of a judge," he begins weakly. Then, with a sudden hot scorn of what looks like a shirking of a confession of the faith for which he would so gladly die, he burns his ships, adding emphatically: "But, yes, she *is* pretty—extraordinarily pretty!"

"*Extraordinarily!*" repeats Euphemia, lifting her eyebrows. "Well, that is more than I should have expected. There are so few people who are *extraordinarily* pretty."

"Who is extraordinarily pretty?" asked Lady Bramshill, beginning to discover that her social baits, her attempts to revive Green Leigh associations, and her exertions for the bettering of Mrs. Clarence's lot, are all falling on deaf ears. "You excite our curiosity—do not they, Lucy? Who is extraordinarily pretty?"

"Honor Lisle! at least, so Mr. Clarence says," with a faint coloring of doubt.

"Honor Lisle! Honor Lisle still! We are getting quite tired of Honor Lisle!"

"Well, if you do not like our conversation, we will relieve you of it," cries Euphemia gayly, springing out of her hammock. "Come, Mr. Clarence; they are not worthy of our theme. We will pursue it in peace among the peaches."

He obeys her only too gladly, the irksomeness of the situation beginning to grow unbearable to him.

"What a fine, strapping couple they are!" cries Lady Bramshill admiringly, watching the retreating figures. A few hours ago the expression would have grated on Mrs. Clarence's ear; now she hears it with indifference. It is not with the blonde giantess who is leading him off that her own doom lies. "Do you expect to keep him long with you this time?"

Mrs. Clarence starts. Her mind is so occupied by the dreadful fear that has stormed into it, memory and intelligence are so absorbed in piecing together the scraps of ominous information she has overheard, that the harmless question put to her gains a sinister and quite unintended meaning.

"Keep him with me!" she repeats vaguely.

"Yes. I mean, will he spend most of the vacation with you?"

"He is thinking of taking me a little trip abroad—

at least "—with an inward pang at the idea of a possible, nay, probable, change of plan—" at least, he *was.*"

"What sort of a traveler are you? Somehow I cannot fancy you much of a traveler. I feel sure that you are the sort of person who always takes her own sheets and pillow-cases with her."

"I do not think I am a very bad one!" with a small and depressed attempt at self-assertion. "I am always ready in time, and I do not make much fuss. Harry has never complained of me."

"Do you take a maid?"

"No."

"You dress your own hair?"

"Yes. It does not need much dressing; it is only twisted. I do it myself, and if I am very tired Harry does it for me."

Another sharper pang at the thought that in the near future—so quickly have her fears sprung to meet the coming evil—she will have to forego these tender ministrations.

"Why, he is son and daughter in one to you!" cries her friend, with rough good-nature.

"Yes; he is everything in the world to me!"

It is with a sort of melancholy superstition that she makes this statement; a kind of dim hope that, by putting before the unseen powers her utter nakedness of all comfort and help save what lies in her son, they may avert or suspend the blow that is threatening her.

When the spread tea-table and the claret-cup reunite the party, Harry sees, by the plaintive on-one-sidedness of his mother's head and the extreme smallness of her voice—never a very large one—how little enjoyment she is deriving from the outing. It is late, however,—nearing dinner-time, from staying to which meal only the most direct statement that they had rather not on the part of Harry has saved them,— when they are allowed to re-enter their fly. Personally, he would have preferred to stay in the cool, wide country spaces rather than re-enter the strait and sultry town, to defer the dreaded hour of the now unavoidable explanation—inevitable, thanks to his own clumsy and needless dissembling.

Nor can Abigail quite conceal her regret at being reft from the society of the now tamed and warmly intimate Adolphus, who has gone far to reconcile her to the rural scenes which she so cordially detests. But the tense weariness of his mother's whole air, honestly as she tries to hide it, warns the son, who all his life has so lovingly studied the weather-glass of her looks, to resist the blandishments of the hostess. So far is Mrs. Clarence from having any share in her own deliverance that she steals a wistful look for direction as to the form of response her son would wish her to make to the bombardment of affectionate entreaties and bribes with which Lady Bramshill is cannonading her. It is a look which does not escape Miss Euphemia.

"He has got his womankind in rare good order," she says, as they stand on the damp-growing sward watching the guests' departure. "Did you see the piteous looks that they turned upon him for orders as to what course he wished them to take about your invitation? I must say I sympathized with him in his determination not to stay—brutally as he expressed it—and dine in his morning clothes this weather. But oh, mother, how *could* you have said that the boys would supply him with dress clothes? What is there in the wardrobe of all those dear little pygmies that could be-stretched to cover the area of that gigantic prig?"

"Is he a prig?" asks Lady Bramshill regretfully, but with interest. "I am sorry to hear you say so. Do you really think that he is a prig?"

"I do not think about it; I *know* that he is."

"I am sorry to hear it."

"You need not be sorry; there are worse things. And I fancy he is a *good* prig; not, indeed, that I ever heard of a *bad* prig. It is the consciousness of overwhelming virtue, I suppose, that makes a man one."

There is a distinct though not very acute asperity in the tone of these remarks which prompts the good-natured mother to take up the cudgels, but with moderation, in defense of the absent.

"I hardly spoke to him, so, of course, you are a much better judge than I; but I liked his manner to his mother—so deferential."

"H'm! I should have said that the deference was more on her side; but, yes, I think he *is* nice to her."

"How did he show his priggishness?"

"How does an Ethiopian show his skin or a leopard his spots?"

Lady Bramshill having no satisfactory answer to this posing question, the subject drops. Meanwhile, the visitors are passing their return comments upon their entertainers.

"I shall never say a word against the country again," breathes out Abigail, in a heartfelt voice. "Oh, what a delightful family!"

Both mother and son laugh. Seldom has the fable of the gold and silver shield met with a better commentary.

"And, oh, *what* order Miss Euphemia keeps her boys in! Adolphus was *so* surprised, almost shocked, when I offered to carry his clubs to the golf-ground because he could not find his caddy. I told him"—ruefully—"that *my* boys always make me carry everything."

"I do not think I see Miss Euphemia carrying anybody's clubs," replies Harry. "She is such a very high and haughty lady."

The obviously deficient admiration which pierces the quasi-playfulness of his tone hits his mother's ear. It strikes her that it was Miss Bramshill's little respectful manner of alluding to the "unknown beloved" which has set her in Harry's black books. With simple subtlety she approaches the subject, her heart beating timorously, under cover, as she thinks, of an apparently careless question.

"Did you not like her manner? I feel sure it is only manner; but it struck me that you did not much admire her tone in speaking of that schoolmate of hers."

For a moment the young man is taken aback at the lamb thus suddenly seizing the bull by the horns. It has never occurred to him as possible that his mother would broach the subject (which will now, thanks to the detestable Euphemia, *have* to be broached) before a third person. He has been bracing his mind for a *tête-à-tête* contest some hours distant, and now the enemy—poor fond enemy!—has sprung upon him in public. A moment's reflection shows him the advantage that treating the burning theme in the necessarily cooling and restraining presence of his young cousin will give him, so he answers as disengagedly as he finds possible:

"You mean the lady whom I met at Mrs. Bevis'?"

"Yes; you know it was the first time I heard of her. You did not mention—you forgot, no doubt, to mention—that there was another lady there besides your hostess."

"Did I? I am almost sure that I told you she had a friend who always came to help her with her harvesting."

"Yes, you did; but I understood it was a man."

"A man!" laughing almost too naturally. "What an absurd mistake! No, it was Miss Lisle. How amused she will be! I must tell her when next we meet."

He adds this last clause advisedly, and casts a hastily anxious glance at his mother, whose eye he has hitherto been avoiding, to see what effect the suggestion of a possible renewal of acquaintance with the unknown object of the terror he so truly and ruefully divines may have upon her. But the shaft misses its aim. She is too preoccupied to make her next question look as artless as she can to heed a

hint which at another time would have made her
shiver with apprehension.

"Is she—this Miss Lisle"—there is a sort of involuntary protest in her way of syllabling the name—
"as—as eccentric as Miss Bramshill represented
her?"

"Eccentric!" he repeats dissatisfiedly; "what is
it to be eccentric? I suppose each one of us must
resign himself to be pelted with the brickbats and
rotten eggs of ugly words, if we dare to swerve a
hair's-breadth from the dusty highroad of convention."

His manner expresses so much indignation, the
tirade is so unnecessarily violent in proportion to the
epithet that has called it forth, that her heart sinks.
He has never run a tilt against convention before.
Is not she herself eminently conventional?

"I do not think 'eccentric' is a very ugly name,
is it?" she says gently. "What I meant to ask
was,—only no doubt I worded it stupidly,—does she
really break in horses and sleep under hedges?"

"It is a ridiculous exaggeration!"—still with that
needless heat—"an absurd misrepresentation! She
never slept under a hedge in her life, and Miss
Euphemia has no business to make such groundless
accusations."

"It would have been no very great crime if she
had slept under a hedge."

The mildness of her tone and the leniency of the
sentiment touch him.

"Eccentric or not eccentric, I am sure that you
would like her—at least, it would be very odd and

unnatural if you did not, since she is strangely like you in appearance."

"Like *me* in appearance? and she breaks in horses and sleeps under haystacks!"

"I do not say that she is like you in tastes and habits; but she is curiously like you in looks—the same arch of the head, the same cut of the orbits of the eyes, the same coloring."

"How very curious!" faintly.

"Oddly enough, she has even something of the same quality of voice."

"Indeed!"

"But," laughing uneasily, "she never puts her head on one side when the world weighs heavy upon her."

Mrs. Clarence is conscious that at the present moment her head is at the angle indicated, and she restores it to the perpendicular.

"Is the world weighing heavy upon you just now?" he asks rallyingly, yet caressingly. "I do not know why it should."

"Why do you think it does?" she asks, trying to catch his tone. "I suppose I am a little tired; you know gayety is always a little tiring to a person habitually not gay, and we have been *so* dissipated."

"Yes, haven't we?" echoes Abigail, with a long sigh of retrospective enjoyment. "*What* a delightful afternoon we have had! and here is the dear town beginning again; but I really am not nearly so glad to see it again as I expected I should be. There is a good deal to be said for the country—some country, that is—after all. Is it possible,"—looking eagerly ahead, and with a brief revival of her urban interests,—" that those are the Linley children whom we are going to pass? They surely cannot keep the baby out as late as this? But it *is* they—the imbecile and all in his go-cart!"

Both her companions are relieved by her babble, and the conversation is sedulously kept to the Linley family, about whom Abigail's information is as varied as it is precise, until they reach their own door.

CHAPTER VII.

The first dip into the cold water has been taken. The bugles have sounded the charge, but the battle has not really been engaged. The ice has, however, at least been broken. Thanks, as he feels with regret, to no timely candor of his own, the fact he has been too lacking in moral courage to impart is in his mother's possession. He will, with his own good will, not again approach the subject for some days,—not until it has had time to lose its first rough edge of unwelcome strangeness,—and meanwhile, by subtle allusions and sidelights attractively thrown, he will awake her interest and disarm her prejudices.

To do the latter is, as he is aware, no easy task. The whole shape and frame of her shut-in life have tended to intensify them. In that deep and narrow heart, if the impressions made are few, they are fathomlessly profound. Yet he would not be a lover if all his misgivings were not bottomed by a conviction that, if his enchanting love could but plead her own cause by her mere presence, the victory would be won; that under all the differences so prominently brought out by Euphemia, the two rulers of his heart would recognize their essential likeness to each other. But the millennium is not an event which any of us looks out for to-morrow; and to effect his purpose of drawing together the two lives so essential to him, he must have time—plenty of time. Time is just what one of the essentials seems determined to deny him. It would not be she if she assaulted him by direct attack. Her mild and circuitous advances would be recognized as such only by one who knew her as well as he.

But scarcely has Abigail, happily drowsy after the strong wine of Doll Bramshill's commerce, bid a sleepy good-night and shut the door, before Mrs. Clarence has begun to dig her trenches. And yet he does his hasty best to take the direction of the talk into his own hands.

They are in his study and smoking room—a room less cramped than the narrow exterior of the house would lead one to expect—which "gives" upon a slip of garden, and whither they have descended for Harry to smoke. He is, it is true, at full liberty to blow his clouds as freely as Zeus all over the house. Mrs. Clarence loves the smell of tobacco, with that strong associated love so much more potent than any affection called out by the real merits of the object itself,—because it is connected with her boy,—and which has made countless eyes fond of the ugly, countless ears fond of the discordant, countless noses fond of the unfragrant.

"She is a dear little guest," says Harry, taking another rose-leaf-tipped cigarette from the box beside him, and rushing into hasty encomium of the departed miss, with as little real care for her excellences as it is possible to combine with such an emphasis of appreciation.

"Yes, isn't she? so full of tact. I dare say that

she saw we wanted to talk, and so pretended to be tired."

The young man is conscious that if Miss Dent has discovered any such anxiety in his own case, she must have used a very strong magnifying glass ; but he only says, still with that desperate effort to keep to Abigail :

"I only wish she were not quite so civil ! I do not wonder at Adolphus"—laughing—"being shocked at her determination to fetch and carry for him. Do you notice my frantic and generally unavailing efforts to hinder her waiting, hand and foot, upon me?"

"Yes, she is most obliging ; still, I am glad she is gone. When one wants to talk *really*, it is better to do so *unter vier augen*."

At the present moment Harry would much prefer forty eyes to the four upon which his mother congratulates herself, but he only says :

"How much I wish that you smoked ! Are you *sure* that it would make you sick ? It would be so much more companionable !"

"Do ladies generally smoke now?" she asks, marveling at her own subtlety. "I mean, have you had the idea put into your head lately by seeing any smoking ladies ?"

"I have no reason for supposing that the magnificent Euphemia smokes, if that is what you mean."

It is not in the least what she has meant, of which both are perfectly aware ; but this unexpected parry of her stroke throws her back to her starting point. Her powers of invention are not very great, and it is a matter of two or three minutes before she sets another snare for him, although it wears the aspect of a rejoinder to his last remark :

"Although Lady Bramshill has spoiled her, I fancy that she has been nicely brought up."

He falls into the trap.

"As to that, I think that a good many girls who are nicely brought up smoke—cigarettes, of course—nowadays."

There is a slight heat in his tone, which tells her what she wanted to know—in addition to possessing the tastes of a tramp and a jockey, Honor Lisle smokes! Another silence, scented by the tobacco-flowers, which—suitable blossoms!—are sending in their nightly perfume through the wide-open French windows. He is back in thought in the red-hung *tabagie* at Briarly Cottage, recalling the little shock— so much of his mother's leaven was in him—with which on the first night of her revelation to him he had seen Honor sending two little shafts of smoke through her delicate nostrils ; recalling, too, his subsequent perfect reconcilement to, nay, rapture in, the sight. It seems to him that all the most characteristic self-revealing things she had ever said to him had come through a light veil of smoke—a veil which had emboldened her to bare the harmless secrets of her odd, shy heart to him. But to his mother he can never explain this. It must be by some other side of their two natures that he must try to draw them together.

"You know that my clock is always twenty years behind anyone else's," she says, and her remark steals with strangely discordant effect into his reverie, considering how very softly it is made, "but I never can reconcile myself to the idea of a woman with a pipe in her mouth!"

"A *pipe!*" he echoes, horrified. "Good Heavens! I should think not! You will not find anyone to disagree with you there."

"Shall I not? I did not quite know how fast the world is traveling, its speed has got so far beyond me."

Then, with a pang of fear lest she may be alienating him, freezing up some coming confidence by the touch of bitterness in her tone, she adds humbly:

"I know that I am, without joking, curiously behindhand in my ideas. I do wish you would try to make me a little more what they call 'up to date,' to tell me what really nice people—I know that you have lately been with some *really* nice people—think and feel and do in these kind of matters."

Her humility touches him, coupled with her obvious desire to conquer all her deepest repugnances in order to meet him; touched, too, by the pathos of her transparent stratagem, the little incidental compliment to his Eastshire associates.

"I have no wish for you to cut yourself upon anyone else's pattern," he answers half lightly, yet with emotion; "you do well enough for me as you are; I had rather see other people"—with an involuntary lowering of his voice—"try to cut themselves upon yours. Yet,"—conscious of, and repudiating the falseness of the impression conveyed by this last clause,—"it would make but a botch and a bungle, and, so that there is likeness and sympathy in the main things,—the things that really matter, the everlasting yea and the everlasting nay,—what do a few differences in detail signify?"

This sentence has an oracular air, or would have if it were not thrown out more as a vague reflection than addressed precisely to his auditor. Yet it seems to her so evident an abandonment of his fencing off the subject that she takes her courage in both hands, and makes her first direct assault. But again a few minutes elapse before the battering-ram, so timidly handled, is in working gear.

"Was the lady you met at Briarly Cottage, and whom I so unaccountably mistook for a man, Miss Lisle? How does she spell it, L-i-s-l-e or L-y-l-e?"

"L-i-s-l-e."

"Oh, thanks! Is she—I was going to ask as like me in herself as you describe her to be in person?"

"Not on first acquaintance—not on the surface; but, in the essentials that go to make up the basis of character—the rock on which all else is founded—she is extremely like you. In the first place,"—stroking one of the little white hands, that lies nervously opening and shutting itself on her lap,—" she is very nearly as full of prejudices as you are,"—taking all the sting out of the word by stooping to kiss the hand over which his own had been lovingly passing.

"Am I prejudiced?"

But he is too absorbed to answer, lifted by his theme to the stars.

"And in mind and body she is as high and clean and true."

The mother turns her head aside. Is it because, if his words had not done so, the thrill in his voice would have told her that the ax has fallen?

. . . . .

"The Vaughans have evidently let their house," announces Abigail, from her usual watch-tower at the window next morning.

"Have they?"

A ten days' visit from Miss Dent has perfected her hostess, or she thinks so, in the art of throwing in apparently coherent expressions of assent or dissent to propositions of which she has not heard one word.

"Yes. I see a footman smoking down the area."

"Do you?"

"I cannot think where, in a house of that size, they can put a footman."

"No?"

The tone of the last monosyllable betrays such an apparent inattention that the girl turns her head, and sees Mrs. Clarence puckering vexed brows over an open note. It is an invitation—nay a command, more peremptory than any predecessor—from Lady Bramshill to repeat the visit of yesterday on a larger scale: to come earlier and stay later, eat and drink more, etc.

In the present state of her spirits, which, indeed, always need tender handling, the idea of another enormous afternoon exposed to the kitchen fire, so to speak, of her friend's large assiduities, with no cool springs of inward comfort to refresh her spirit, is intolerably irksome; and yet——

"You would like to go, of course, dear child?"

she says sweetly, yet a little mournfully. "So you shall—so we will, of course. I am afraid we can hardly expect Harry to sacrifice himself again. Ah! here he comes. We will hear what he says."

"What is he supposed to be going to say?"

In answer, she puts the note into his hand.

"Well,"—giving it back to her,—"is there any just cause or impediment?"

"That is for you to decide"—unable to keep a shade of surprise out of her voice. "I thought—I imagined——"

"I suppose"—laughing—"that I ought to give the colossal charms of Miss Euphemia another chance of vanquishing me; and you must confess that this dear little town does not afford any great variety of entertainments. Have you any alternative to suggest?"

"None."

"Then we will certainly go. I will sit at the knees of Miss Euphemia, or as near them as I can reach up, and Abigail shall complete the conquest of Adolphus."

"You may laugh, but he is a very nice boy."

"When once he is retrieved from the bushes," rejoins he teasingly.

His mother had gone docilely to her bureau. He follows her, and lays his hand on her cool gray shoulder.

"What is play to us is death to you, dear. Why should you sacrifice yourself? I saw the extremity of anguish your pleasuring caused you yesterday. Why risk a recurrence? Stay at home, and go to church several times. Judging by the din of your bells, there is never a moment when there is not a function of some kind or other going on in one or other of your joss-houses."

Her pen pauses, and she lifts a doubtful face, half relieved, half hurt. He has never before jeered at her church-going propensities, nor has he ever before proposed to forego her company upon any occasion when it was possible for him to enjoy it. And yet—to be let off!

Her boy's hand is still on her shoulder.

"I will say that you are *indisposed*. In a sense, Heaven knows it is Gospel truth!"

"Had you really rather I did not?"

She herself could not say whether she wishes for "Yes" or "No" to this last question.

"*Much* rather. Do you know that I do not think you realize *how* miserable you look when you are out a-pleasuring."

"Do I? I thought I had hidden my feelings so well."

"And your patient misery makes *me* miserable; so——"

"So I am to be left at home?"

"Yes; you are to be let off your gridiron for to-day. I do not say that you will *every* day."

"*Every day!* Do you mean to go to The Beeches every day?"

"God forbid! I mean, every day that we are to be dragged there."

This phrase implies reluctance, but her surprised ear tells her that there is no real unwillingness. Are his and her thoughts beginning to diverge so widely that he is glad to get away from her even for an afternoon?

Now that she has acquiesced in his arrangement, there is certainly a briskness in his manner which was absent at breakfast.

"I will keep an eye upon Adolphus and Abigail."

"And Adolphus and Abigail will keep an eye upon you and Euphemia," retorts she, delighted, and launching rosily into elemental repartee.

Neither of them expresses any regret at Mrs. Clarence's secession, though Abigail fires off a radiant parting hope that she will not be too dull all alone at home, as they trot off in their hansom—a vehicle for which, since they are only two, they have exchanged yesterday's crawler.

It is not till five minutes after they are gone that the explanation of Harry's readiness to go dawns chilly upon his mother's mind. To Euphemia Bramshill, though otherwise absolutely without charm for him, he will be able to talk of Honor Lisle!

The tone she may take—the tone that his mother yesterday heard her take—about his divinity is not such as to content or do otherwise than irritate him; and yet he had rather be irritated by hearing her unworthily mentioned than do without hearing her spoken of at all.

He is gone to The Beeches to share in a form of festivity which he has always spurned,—a garden party,—and to accept the hospitality of a family for one member of which he has a pronounced distaste, solely because to that one member he can talk of

Honor Lisle. She will be not only in his thoughts, but on his lips, all the afternoon. Here at least—as far as thoughts go—she and her boy will meet, glad as he was to escape her; for she herself thinks of nothing else all day—nothing but Honor Lisle; the girl who smokes, and breaks in horses, and sleeps under haystacks; who can have none of the instincts or feelings of a lady; who has doubtless taught him that new sneer at the religious duties which, if he has not practiced them very rigidly himself, he has always reverenced in his mother: Honor Lisle, in whom— cruelest cut of all—Harry *imagines*—she is very sure that it can exist only in his warped fancy—a likeness to herself, an ironical outside likeness, covering such deep dissimilitude.

Like or unlike, she cannot get away from Honor Lisle. Honor Lisle puts on her bonnet with her, walks downstairs and opens the street door with her, passes along the lifeless street with her, enters the corbeled and gargoyled western door of St. Michael's Church with her, sits on the next *prie-dieu* to her through the intoned and chanted evensong, makes nonsense of her prayers and a mockery of her praises, and, finally, insists on walking home with her.

Would not one naturally hate a person who pursued one with so relentless a persecution? The passion of hatred has had so small a part in her life that she scarcely knows or can recognize its aspect. She is only heavily conscious that all day long something ugly and frightening is creeping on hands and knees into her heart. It has so long to do it in, too, for the absentees do not return till the high-swinging bells in the dusking belfries are ringing the curfew. They come in with a sort of whiff of the country still clinging to them—Abigail with her hands full of hot-house flowers and her mouth of blissful babble.

"Lady Bramshill sends you these. She gathered them herself, though she seemed a good deal afraid of the gardener, and there is one—a California—which, she said, he would kill her if he found out that she had been cutting; but, all the same, she is going to tell him to send you flowers twice a week. She was so sorry you could not come. She asked so much about you, and wanted to know how long it is since you have been such an invalid."

"An *invalid!*" growing a little pink. "I am no invalid!"

"Oh, but do not you remember you told us to say that you were *indisposed?* And when she asked if you would come with us to-morrow, Harry looked very grave, and said he feared you might still be *indisposed.* I was so afraid of catching his eye and laughing, but it answered perfectly. Lady Bramshill was not in the least offended, and yet she will not expect you."

"You are going, then, again to-morrow?"

The question is addressed to that one of the truants who has not hitherto spoken, and is sent gently to him on a serene and quite happy-looking smile, which, if he did but know it, goes far to disprove his own assertion of her want of power to disguise her feelings.

She is dressed even more prettily than usual, in a gown that her son helped her to choose, and perhaps for that reason, though he has forgotten the circumstance, never sees without commending. The ugly guest that has sat at her heart's hearth all her long day has left at least no trace of his visit on the sweet smallness of her face. She has always liked her own beauty, because of his pride in it. Perhaps now it will help her to win back the ground she lost last night by her defect of sympathy with him.

"Unless you can rescue us," he answers.

"I could not fulfill my promise of keeping an eye upon Harry and Euphemia," cries Abigail, bubbling over into giggles, "because they disappeared somewhere together for nearly the whole afternoon. Lady Bramshill grew quite fidgety about them."

It has seemed to the covertly watching mother that, though it is only her son's back from which she can draw inferences, since he is just walking off to dress, at Abigail's indiscretion even his shoulders have an annoyed look.

"I dare say that they had pleasant things to talk about—that they found interesting subjects to discuss in common," rejoins she, with soft haste.

By the tone of her voice and the shape of her sentence she would fain convey to him both a knowledge of what the theme she hints at must have been and a willingness to approach it conciliatorily. In a sense she succeeds, for at the door he turns, and, showing a brow which, though obviously lately cloudy, is as apparently now clearing, answers pretty cheerfully :

"We bickered a good deal. She is a girl whom one would always bicker a good deal with. I like a *pillowy* woman."

The fiction of Mrs. Clarence's invalidhood is successfully maintained during the remaining week of Abigail Dent's visit, and her friend Lady Bramshill is too much occupied by her gigantic brood, their cricket suppers and their impending transplantation to the seaside, to be able to verify in person the reports of her indisposition; she has to content herself with a storm of notes, vegetables, names of London doctors to be consulted and local ones to be shunned. But the young people meet repeatedly. Between the estimate of the family at The Beeches formed by Harry and that by Abigail Dent, a mean is more nearly being arrived at than at first seemed probable.

Abigail has had some illusions to lose, in the discovery that a further acquaintance with Adolphus reveals more likeness to her own boys in the matter of a willingness to run her off her legs in his service, than the fine veneer of his early manner, under Euphemia's eye, had led her to expect. Harry, on the other hand, if he never says much in praise of Euphemia, has ceased to gird at her height or her autocracy.

At the close of a second garden party at The Beeches, during which Miss Bramshill's aid to her parent has been conspicuously wanting, and her presence not conspicuously present, Lady Bramshill meets her daughter sauntering leisurely homeward across the gravel just furrowed by the latest wheel.

"Where *have* you been?" she asks, with that natural irritability which the sight of cool slim idleness must breed in the breast of toiling fat. "I have been looking for you everywhere. Mrs. Fraser wanted to see the things that are over from the bazaar, and the prices had come off some of them, and I am sure I undercharged her shamefully for that pokerwork screen. Where *can* you have been?"

"And how can you have made yourself so astonishingly hot wondering about such a very simple thing?" replies Euphemia, looking with an unfeigned, if rather superior, compassion at her mother. "I was sitting in the boathouse with Harry."

"Harry? What Harry? Harry who?"

"Harry Clarence. Who else?"

"H'm!"

"He tried to scull me up the river, but the weeds were so thick we could not get along,—I must really speak to Felton about having it cleared out,—so we came back and sat in the boathouse."

"H'm!"

"Why do you go on saying 'H'm'?"

There is that note of lofty rebuke in the daughter's voice before which Lady Bramshill is wont to bow a subdued and suppliant head; but her wrongs and her temperature have apparently made her less tractable than usual.

"I go on saying 'H'm,'" replies she, with fire, "because I do not think it was very kind of you to leave me to bear the whole burden of entertaining seventy people, with the thermometer at eighty-nine in the shade."

"In the sun, you mean," correcting her mother's error with a cool moderation which exasperates that mother still further.

"Nor do I see why you need have entirely monopolized one of our very few young men."

Euphemia's well-drawn eyebrows rise a little in unaffected surprise at this most unwonted strain of scolding. It gives her a slight feeling of titillated amusement.

"Why should not I? Nobody else wanted him."

Lady Bramshill is so much in the habit of being nonplused by her daughter that to this question, though there are half a dozen good answers to it, she gives none.

"Most girls like each other better than men nowadays," continues Euphemia; "and as to Abigail Dent, so as she has somebody's boots to lick, it is not of the least consequence whose."

"What you could find to say to him all those hours passes my comprehension."

"Does it?"

"You began by calling him a prig."

"Yes."

"You began by saying that he was a gigantic prig."

"One seldom ends quite where one began, does one?"

The words are ambiguous, but the tone is so teasing, and the smile at her lip-corners so unimpassioned and so sly, that a partial reassurance comes to the mother. But it is only partial, and she still feels extremely hot.

"I know," she says, with the normal pride in her progeny bursting through the evanescent ire, "that there is not a girl in Europe better able to take care of herself than you; but you must remember that you are only eighteen, and also that you ought to think of him."

"I think of him very often."

"You say that only to plague me," fanning herself with the programme of the band music, for it has been a Blue Hungarian function.

"I do not. I say it because it is true. I do think of him a good deal."

"Then all I can say is, you had better begin to leave off thinking of him as quickly as you can."

There is so much more brusque earnestness in her manner than seems to her daughter warranted by the occasion, that she unbuttons two protesting eyes and asks:

"Why?"

"Because"—with energy—"there is not anyone in the whole circle of our acquaintance whom you can think of less profitably—think of, that is, in the sense which the word generally bears in a girl's mouth."

"I do not know anything about other girls' mouths; in mine it means exactly the same as it does in the dictionary."

"Very well, very well!" retorts Lady Bramshill, breaking the back of the programme in the energy of her oscillation. "You can always get the better of me because you are so much cleverer, better educated."

"I do not think"—laughing in good-humored surprise—"that I have given any evidence of oppressively high culture in the conversation so far."

"But I know what I mean."

"It is more than I do. A week ago there was nothing too good for you to say of the man: his manners to his mother, the color of his hair, the way he picked up your pocket handkerchief—everything he did became him in the doing."

"I do not go back from a word of it. I am sure he is an out-and-out good fellow, and his mother worships his very shadow."

There is a slight tincture of remorse in the tone of the last words, which emboldens the never-wanting-in-boldness Euphemia to throw her bombshell.

"Then, if I have fastened, or am intending to fasten, my young affections upon him, what, in Heaven's name, is there to hinder me?"

The effect of a bombshell is often almost as startling to the thrower as to the object aimed at, nor is the present case an exception.

"*What is there to hinder you?*" repeats Lady Bramshill, with a shocked emphasis which has very apparently nothing fictitious about it. "How little you know what you are talking about! If I thought that there was the least chance of *that*, how bitterly I should regret having ferreted out poor Lucy!"

"I fancy that she regrets it already," replies Euphemia, in puzzled mirth, "since you have robbed her of her son's company, and sent her more vegetable marrows than anyone could eat in the course of the longest life."

"Where is Abigail?" asks Adolphus, coming up at this point, and rescuing his mother for the moment from that pursuit of the enigmatic subject upon which his sister is bent.

"*Abigail!*" repeats Euphemia reprovingly. "My dear boy, do you think that that is the proper way of speaking of a young lady behind her back?"

"It is the way in which I speak to the young lady to her face," replies Adolphus, but, like his mother, less docilely than usual; "she asked me to call her Abigail."

"The way in which you put upon that poor girl is really too bad!" says Lady Bramshill, unconsciously solaced by finding someone on whom safely to vent the irritation of her spirit, and making the innocent Adolphus pay for his sister's guilt. "I saw her yesterday positively *staggering* under the weight of your fishing-tackle."

"I cannot help it," replies Adolphus gloomily. "I never saw such a girl—she says she *likes* carrying things. I have tried to stop her, but I cannot. Yes, Euphemia, you may laugh, but I have. She has always been getting me into trouble with you ever since the first day when you dragged me out of the bushes. I wish she had never come near the place!"

He disappears, as always, deferential to his sister, but with lacerated feelings.

CHAPTER VIII.

Unconscious of the torch of discord that her too great obsequiousness has lit at The Beeches, Abigail sings her nightly pæan in praise of the family there to patient, but rather tired, ears.

Harry sings no pæan, but he continues to frequent their society.

His mother suffers none of the apprehensions that are beginning to disturb Lady Bramshill; that would have tormented herself, had not a bigger cloud of dread wiped off all the little foolish cloudlets of baseless fear that were wont to fleck her firmament. She would not even grudge the loss of his society—has she ever grudged him anything?—if she could think it was only the innocent delight taken by the young in the young that has robbed her of his company. But the gravity of his face, in moments when he thinks himself sheltered from her observation, tells her that it is the fact of his having for the first time in his life a trouble,—or, at least, an absorbing interest,—which he is unable to share with her, that makes him happier out of than in her presence.

There is a slight, gossamer-slight veil being drawn between their hearts. She compares it in her own mind to the cataract slowly growing over an eye— a thin, imperceptibly thin, skin to begin with, ending in total darkness.

With bitter self-reproach she tells herself that it is her own fault: the result of that senseless, lifelong jealousy of whose existence he is as well aware as she herself. How long ago did she begin to be jealous of him, she asks herself, sitting lonely in the little back garden under her plum tree, and looking vacantly at the tobacco blossoms—brown, dead-looking, and shabby in their daylight *dishabille*. She was jealous—sick-jealous; jealous even to dismissal of his nurse Nasmyth, old and valuable servant as she was; jealous of the button-nosed baby who sat on the bench at the kindergarten beside him. But she has never been really jealous before.

Daily that creeping hatred—hatred of an unseen, unknown object, yet none the less hatred—steals further into her heart. The ugly, unaccustomed inmate frightens her. She has been so little used to hate anyone! The discovery that she is capable of it fills her with a sense of her deep depravity.

Her form of religion is one that has led her to find comfort in confession, and as upon the door of St. Michael's Church hangs one of those—a little disingenuous—announcements that some of the clergy will be to be found in the church between the hours of two and four, she has been in the habit of availing herself of it, to clear her spirit from the stain of her tiny peccadilloes.

How much more, then, ought she to acknowledge and do penance for a sin of so much deeper a dye! But it is infinitely difficult to her to bring herself to the accomplishment of this, to her, so obvious duty. What if the penance imposed be that of receiving with open arms—and even going to meet—the calamity that threatens her?

It is not till the day of Abigail's departure that she nerves herself to the execution of her task. Her son has gone to see off at the station the tearful girl, who is leaving St. Gratian with several street problems unsolved.

As Mrs. Clarence issues from the church her son joins her. He sees her before she sees him. The last week's mental struggle has told upon her, or is it the shadow of the porch from which she emerges that throws a sickly light upon her?

"I knew that you were a safe find here," Harry says, smiling, and yet with a tinge of annoyance in his tone. "How pale you look! I suppose you have been kneeling for hours upon that hard, cold pavement?"

"Indeed I have not. I had a hassock."

They are walking down the little sleepy thoroughfare, where there is no incommoding jostle, nor much noise of wheels to make talk difficult.

"Well, did she set off all right?"

"She was a little sniffy, poor child! but consoled by chocolates out of a slot."

"I am afraid you will miss her."

"I am quite sure I shall not."

There is so much energy in the denial that the idea at once flashes across his mother's mind—perennially occupied by one idea—that he has been waiting the departure of the visitor to embark with herself upon the shunned theme, which yet both feel to be so near. The thought takes her breath away. Is the strength of the holy resolutions that she has been so devoutly and heartfeltly framing in the confessional to be put so quickly to the proof? At least, it must not be in the open street.

They reach home with scarcely another word exchanged, and pass straight through the house to the plum tree, under whose shade two Turkey-red-covered bamboo chairs await and receive them.

Mrs. Clarence's head feels hot. She would like to take off her hat, but the mechanical habit of a lifetime, which has now the strength of an instinct,—the habit of never letting her boy see her at anything but the highest pitch of dainty neatness,—checks the impulse. There might be a hair or two out of place, and "a sweet disorder in the dress" is lovely only in early youth. She does not formulate the thought, but it keeps her hatted. No such consideration need or does affect the young man. He throws off his hat, and leans back, with one hand holding his temples, and with its fingers wrinkling the skin of his forehead.

"Have you a headache?"

"Not in the least. I was only thinking."

The easy, natural question, "Thinking of what?" would probably arrive at the core of the matter, but it is not put.

"I was thinking how convenient it would be occasionally to be able to be in two places at once, like a bird."

She looks gently interrogative.

"I have been springing a little surprise upon you. You know that I went to London a day or two ago.

Well, it was to visit Mr. Cook, and take tickets for our trip down the Loire. I thought that as soon as we had shunted Abigail you would be ready to start."

A little billow of color, slight and delicate, like everything else about her, washes over Mrs. Clarence's face. During the last week the Loire has seemed a more distant stream than Abana and Pharpar, rivers of Damascus.

"I am always ready to start in five minutes, as you know,"—with a low, happy laugh,—" or, indeed, at a pinch, in two and a half."

"And now I perversely get by this afternoon's post an invitation for the same time; an invitation which"—a moment's hesitation—"I should have rather liked to accept."

He has drawn an envelope from his pocket, and half, but only half, holds it out to her. Since it is only half offered, honor bids her feign not to see the overture, but out of the corner of her eye she detects an Eastshire postmark.

"It is a bore when pleasant things clash, isn't it?" he asks.

His persistence shows her that he wishes to be questioned, though the letter has slidden back into his pocket.

"It is from—whom?"

"From Mrs. Bevis."

She had known it, and yet she cannot help a slight start, which makes the bamboo of her chair rustle.

"Why, you left her only ten days ago!"

His head is stooped over the yellow kitchen cat,

who has stepped out of the area to greet him, and whose long upright tail he is smoothing from root to tip. The sensation is none the less agreeable to her that he is unaware of causing it.

"It is about that recreation room which was the primary object of my visit, and which we forgot all about; or, rather, we were too busy with the harvest"— a luxury of recollection in his voice. "And now the well-known philanthropist, Henderson, has promised to run down to her, and she wants me to meet him, and give her the benefit of my legal knowledge as to a disputed point about the land."

Human nature asserts its sway. So it seems the Loire is still to be classed with Abana and Pharpar for her. She cannot speak.

"Of course, in the case of a man so much occupied as Henderson, one must take him when one can get him; and besides, as Mrs. Bevis says, she knows that as soon as the Courts begin to sit again, *I* shall be tied."

"Will Mr. Cook take back the tickets, or shall we be obliged to forfeit them? Perhaps if I knew what sort of a traveler Abigail would make, I might take her with me instead of you."

There is a creditably tiny quiver in her voice, but there is no huff. Perfect love, among the many things besides fear which it casts out, excludes huff.

Her son detects the tremble. He drops the yellow cat's tail, a desistence which she receives with a strident mew of displeasure, and lays his hand on his mother's daintily gloved one, which she never exposes to sun tan.

"You are in a prodigious hurry to dismiss me. Abigail would make a terrific fellow-traveler; she would be the death of you in a week, and I decline to be thrown away like an old glove after all my years of faithful couriership."

She looks at him as if doubting her own good fortune, doubting, too, whether, even if it be within her reach, she dare seize it.

"I only want you to do what you like best, and you know that the Loire, though it is always running, will not run away. We can go there next——"

She cannot finish the sentence. She knows that if Harry steam past Blois and Chenonceaux and Amboise next year, it will be with Honor by his side. If there were still any selfish hesitation in his heart, that half-finished sentence ends it.

"What have I always liked best? Pack your trunk; we set off on Monday."

"My *trunk!*"—between laughing and crying—"that sounds like one of those dreadful hair things that servants used to have in my youth. And what about Eastshire?"

"Eastshire be hanged!"

It is the nearest approach to the heroic he has ever made in all his twenty-eight years. "Eastshire be hanged!" The phrase recurs with reassuring force to Mrs. Clarence during the ensuing foreign trip whenever the idea strikes her that that trip is not quite what former ones had been. It would be hard to her to say in what the difference lies. But that there is a subtle one, she tries in vain to disprove to herself. The weather is admirable, her own punctuality as impeccable, and her son's approbation of it as sincere, and as openly expressed, as ever. They come upon pleasant people, of whom they see enough, and not too much, and yet—— The spirit seems to have evaporated out of the vial.

For the first time in their lives, both are glad when the holiday ends. Harry is gladder still when the Law Courts resume their sittings. On the first day of his resumption of work his mother notices an alerter tone in his voice on his return than had been observable since his Eastshire visit.

"Well?"

"Well, how have you been getting on?"

"Oh, I saw Blair, and White, and Harvey. Blair has been to Chicago, and White has been to Roumania, and Harvey has had a river in Norway. Very poor sport; an extraordinarily dry year."

"I do not care where they have been, or what they have been doing. What I want to know is, what *you* have been doing to-day?"

"I! Oh, I have been in rather an amusing case: a grocer bringing an action for libel against a novelist because he made one of his characters in a novel describe his (the tradesman's) goods as 'shoddy.'"

"And were they shoddy?"

"Undoubtedly; but that would not affect the libel."

"Were you for the plaintiff or the defendant?"

"For the plaintiff."

"For the shoddy grocer?" lifting her eyebrows.

"Yes; old Hodgins was my leader. He opened

the case, and then he had to go off to another he was engaged in in the Court of Appeal."

" And you were in—what court ? "

" Queen's Bench. I went on with the case. I had to examine the witnesses ; some amusing things came out."

" What sort of things ? "

But Mrs. Clarence is destined never to hear what flowers of forensic humor adorned the case of Stokes *versus* Nokes, for at this moment her son's eye falls upon a letter which the entering servant is tendering him, and which, after one glance at the superscription, he tears open. She sees his face fall as he reads, and the gesture of thrusting the document into his pocket, on meeting the solicitude of her eye, gives her an inkling of whence it comes.

" You were asking me—*what?*" he says, with an obvious effort to recover wits which have plainly strayed far enough afield.

" I was asking you what the sort of amusing things were which came out."

" Stupid of me ! I cannot recall any special one at this moment. They will come back to me in the course of the evening."

" I hope "—very hesitatingly—" that you have not had bad news ? "

" No-o ! oh, dear no ! My letter, if that is what you allude to, is only a business one."

She must have been mistaken in thinking that she had descried that Eastshire postmark.

" At least, it is only relating to Mrs. Bevis' recreation room."

Then her eyes had not deceived her.

"It will be no recreation room to you by the time you have done with it. Will you be able to squeeze out a day or two from your courts? Your Sundays, at all events, are free ; and from what you tell me of her, Mrs. Bevis is not, I fancy, a very strict Sabbatarian."

"She does not want me to go there ; she only asks for my written opinion."

"Indeed !"

"She could not receive me, for the excellent reason that she will not be at home herself. She is off almost immediately to India."

"Alone ? What an enterprising lady she must be !"

"Not quite alone. Miss Lisle goes with her."

Once already a messenger has come galloping up to Mrs. Clarence's gallows' foot with a reprieve in his hand, but it is not usual for such a thing to happen twice. Safe for a whole winter ! Safe from insidious projects of philanthropy veiling cruel designs against her peace ! Safe from shrimping and barebacked horse riding, and from the whole battery of unladylike yet incomprehensibly beguiling artillery that has been leveled against him ! The evil thought, that wears almost the face of a hope, of how many perils beset even the easy path of the traveler of to-day flashes across her mind, with the other thought hard upon its heels, of how ugly a figure the mere admission of such a half hope will cut when she next kneels at the confessional. But not even the remorseful pang that accompanies her recognition of the wickedness of her own heart can go near to quell the thrill of joy with which she repeats over and over to herself, "For the winter he is safe."

It goes placidly by : soft-weathered, and cut off at both ends by a late tarrying autumn and a hurrying spring. It seems to her the shortest she has ever known. The mildness of the weather does not in reality abridge the Indian travelers' absence, yet it gives the impression of having done so. It is behind them. Easter, too, with its recess, has now spun past, and before you can "crier gare " summer and a latish Whitsun are upon the world.

The two Orientals must have returned long ere this, yet no tidings of their having done so reach slumbrous St. Gratian; no note of invitation or inquiry or mere greeting arrives from Eastshire—at least, not to Mrs. Clarence's knowledge ; and she is certain that an intuition would make her at once divine on her boy's face, in the timbre of his voice, and his very gait, the glow and thrill and electric life which any communication, any renewed connection, with that not very inspiring county would lend him.

But for this conviction, his much more frequently than formerly remaining in London for a night or two to fulfill evening engagements might inspire her with suspicion. But she knows that upon the countenance of those who have been face to face with their God a betraying luster must always linger, and upon his, when he returns to her, there is none. He is as loving as ever, perhaps even a little more demonstratively so than he used to be, and busy, the illustrious Hodgins having continued to put work in his way ;

but there is no radiance about him. His increased tenderness of manner would lift her to the skies if it were not spoiled by the suspicion that it is due to the likeness he has imagined in her to the absent object of her dread. She would like—oh, how earnestly!—to amputate, as it were, from his kind looks all that does not honestly belong to her.

Between the Bramshills and the little household at St. Gratian, for one reason or another, there has been less communication than the first ardor of their intercourse would lead one to expect. It is possible that Lady Bramshill's fears about the son may have lessened her desire to extract the mother from her shell, or the hopelessness of the task rebutted her; and Harry's own willingness to frequent The Beeches —always of a rather spurious quality—seems to have been exchanged for an occasional careless call of civility.

Euphemia has, since Mrs. Clarence discovered the true lie of the land in her son's heart, never been an object of jealousy to her; yet she is glad that even his false and second-hand relish for her society has died out. There had never been but one topic of common interest between them,—that of Honor Lisle, —and it is evidence, almost too reassuring to be believed, of his growing indifference to the subject that he no longer seeks the company of the one with whom alone he could discuss it.

Whitsun has come, and even slow St. Gratian has felt in some degree the titillation of its festivity. Large posters adorn its blank walls, announcing the advent, for one night only, of the world-famous Miss

Poppy de Vere, of the Popularity Theater. The young lady in question, besides being a danseuse of the highest caliber, has the additional attraction of being the consort of a *real* nobleman, whose coronet she sprinkles, with that liberality which marks her whole character, over her stage properties.

The dancing might have left St. Gratian cold, being a staid and serious-minded little town; but the opportunity of seeing a countess skip for hire is one which its inhabitants cannot resist, and every place is taken in the usually slackly attended, and, by the better sort, contemned, little theater. The stage-box is occupied by as many of the Bramshill family as can fit into it, and such as cannot have boiled over into the next one.

Their party is swelled by three guests—the junior curate of St. Michael's, whom, palpitating and protesting, Lady Bramshill has compelled to come in; a sparkling Indian widow, an old flame of the judge's; and a young girl.

"It is packed to the ceiling!" says Lady Bramshill, in a tone of self-gratulation. "I do like a full house! What a pity that better companies do not come here generally! It is really not a bad little theater."

"I cannot conceive what could have made it worth Poppy de Vere's while to come here, all the same," replies Euphemia wonderingly, "or why her manager allowed her."

"From what I have heard of her, I should think she was about as likely to ask her manager's leave as she would his lordship's," says the widow, with an air of private information. "I suppose that she will, of course, be very late as usual. She kept the audience at the Popularity waiting a good half hour one night. Someone in the pit actually hissed her when she came on; and when she did appear, it was with one blue and one pink shoe. Of course, she was a little elevated!"

To this edifying account of the habits and natural history of the latest addition to the British peerage the two girls, being girls of to-day, listen with the most perfect equanimity, not even enlivened by interest or surprise, since they knew it all before.

The widow has to turn her batteries upon the curate, to whom she imparts in an undertone anecdotes of the danseuse's past history — rather an accentuated one. He is so shocked and ashamed that, though the atmosphere is stifling, he keeps on his mackintosh throughout the performance, in his endeavors to conceal his cloth.

"Do you see anyone that you know, Honor?" asks Euphemia, in a low tone, of her girl guest; "I mean, do you recognize any friend?"

The eyes of the person addressed are at the moment fixed upon the corresponding box to that occupied by the Bramshill party on the other side of the theater—a box in which two persons, a young man and a young woman, have just seated themselves.

"I see a Mr. Clarence, whom I met last year in Eastshire," replies the other quietly.

The answer has been preceded by a hesitation so minute as to escape even Euphemia's keen ears.

"*A Mr. Clarence!*" repeats she indignantly. "Is that all you have to say about him? Is this all the outcome of the surprise I have so cleverly sprung upon you?"

Miss Lisle's eyes have not, after the first glance, again resorted to their *vis-à-vis*. They turn calmly to her friend.

"I do not see where the surprise comes in. I knew that Mr. Clarence lived at St. Gratian."

"There is Harry Clarence," says Lady Bramshill, touching her daughter's arm with her fan, "chaperoning that little cousin of his, Miss What's-her-name. So she is staying with them again. Very good-natured of him. Not but what I dare say it is one word for her and two for himself. Ha, ha! How lazy of Lucy not to bring the girl herself! I shall tell her so next time we meet. Or what do you say to our going and *drawing* her after the play? It will not be very late, because, of course, we will only stay for Poppy's last dance. Shall we make her— Lucy, I mean—give us a glass of claret and a sandwich? What do you say? I call it an inspiration!"

Euphemia shrugs her shoulders.

"You will probably have to *draw* her out of bed!"

The disapproval indicated by her tone is not so marked as that with which she often salutes her mother's inspirations, and her parent goes on:

"I will broach the idea to Harry when he comes round to speak to us. If he smiles upon it,—and I am sure he will,—I do not, without joking, see any reason why we should not carry it out."

Euphemia refrains from either assent or dissent, and a moment later the curtain rises; and though the crowning glory of the evening is not to appear till the middle of the first act, yet the expectation of her imminent advent keeps eyes and ears on the alert.

CHAPTER IX.

When at length Poppy, Countess of Camelot, beams on the sight, blazing in jewels other than Cornelia's, and floats across the stage with that graceful mixture of the feather and the serpent which, in combination— if fame wrong her not—with a command of bad language unrivaled in the greenrooms of Europe, has danced her into possession of lands that date from Bosworth, what room can there be in the breasts of her audience for aught but reverent and breathless admiration of so consummate a product of our age? And when the curtain falls after the first act, what topic has any chance in competition with her? The highest pitch of enthusiasm is, perhaps, reached by the Indian widow, who is heard relating to the curate how a great social authority had said that Poppy de Vere's legs were a poem!—an anecdote which makes the unfortunate young man hug his suffocating cloak as closely as did the east wind in the fable the traveler his.

When the second act and interact are over, Lady Bramshill wakes from the trance of admiration which she has shared with the rest of the house to a more everyday topic :

"I cannot think why Harry Clarence has not been round to speak to us. Did he make you out, Honor? He is an old friend of yours, isn't he? If he did, how very odd that he does not come to renew acquaintance! But perhaps the curtain hides you. Do sit a little more forward."

"I do not think there is any need," replies the girl politely, but with a slight, reluctant smile; "we bowed to each other some little time ago."

"Oh, that is all right! I suppose he does not like to leave his cousin. Very absurd of him; but he is such a formal old thing! Only children are always either grossly ill or oppressively well mannered! Have you ever noticed that?"

"I do not know that I have"—slowly.

Euphemia makes a sign of disapprobation to her mother, behind the guest's back, of the slight disparagement implied in her last remark.

"Mother naturally does not relish manners whose goodness brings home to her the unlicked condition of her own cubs!" she says, with a laugh.

Lady Bramshill, though mystified by her daughter's frown, and not much relishing this partisanship, yet from the force of habit, and because her spirit, except under the stress of very unusual circumstances, always stands rebuked before her child's, hastens to acquiesce:

"Indeed, I dare say there may be something in that."

But, whether due to the excess of his homage to the humble Abigail, or to whatever other cause, it is clear, as the evening goes on, that Mr. Clarence has no intention of paying his respects to his friends in their box. When he leaves the theater, which is a few minutes before the Bramshill party get under way, it is in company with his cousin.

His conduct excites in Lady Bramshill's mind a voluble astonishment mixed with inconsistent indignation. It is inconsistent since she ought to be glad at a trait which so clearly proves the young man's indifference toward her daughter. When, on reaching the delightful freshness of the open air, she finds that her carriage is not at once forthcoming, the intention she had earlier in the evening expressed of "drawing" Mrs. Clarence—an intention then only half serious—takes solid consistence.

"Doll shall go to the Swan and see what has happened,—this sort of thing always comes to pass if one does not bring a footman,—and we will ask Lucy to take us in and give us something to eat. The theater always makes me ravenous; does not it you, Euphemia?"

Miss Bramshill offers no resistance to the project, whatever her private opinion of its tactfulness may be, and Honor's protest is so softly uttered that it goes quite unheeded. Honor has been so much used all her life to acquiesce in actions and projects which she dislikes that she has become a past-mistress in the art of concealing her emotions. No one who saw the serenity of her serious eyes and the sweet civility of her smile would guess the profound distaste and shrinking with which she is driven into sharing this injudicious forcing of the privacy of one whose first impression of her she would so fain have had a favorable one. And worse—far worse than the suffering caused by this intrusion on his mother, is the wound from which her deep, shy pride bleeds at thus brazenly going to seek one who had so plainly shunned her.

At first it seems as if she were to escape the ordeal, through the fact of their being unable to gain admittance. The house stands black and silent among its black and silent neighbors, lifting its little smokeless chimney-stack to the starred canopy of the night.

"They have gone to bed! It is all shut up!" says Euphemia, surveying the frontage. "There is not even a light in the area!"

"It *is* a little late, isn't it?" puts in Honor. "I heard the church clock strike half-past twelve as we came by."

But no one who hears the calmness of the tiny protest would guess the ardor of prayer for its success in turning the leader of the expedition from her insensate purpose with which it is uttered. It has the fate of many other prayers.

"Impossible!" cries Lady Bramshill, returning with fresh vigor to the bell-pull; "Harry and little Miss What's-her-name must at all events be up. Why, they were not three minutes ahead of us; and"—her thoughts reverting fondly to the thought of refreshment—"they could not go to bed without something to eat. Ah, I thought so! Here comes somebody at last!"

The "somebody" is a distrustful maid-servant, who opens the door parsimoniously and on the chain, and looks doubtfully out.

"It is all right!" cries the leader of the invaders jubilantly. "You may let us in. We are not burglars. We are only four hungry ladies come to ask for a sandwich. Your mistress is not gone to bed?

No! I thought not. Ah!"—turning a triumphant look over her shoulder at her followers as she crosses the threshold—"who was right now?"

To one of those followers, who steps along reluctant and hindmost, they seem dreadfully numerous, voluminous, impertinent, as they rustle along a narrow passage to the back den on the ground floor, for which, when her son spends an evening at home, Mrs. Clarence forsakes her own prettier and more cheerful domain.

Terribly intrusive they seem as she catches sight of the little family tableau during the second before the three persons who compose it become aware of their presence. It is clear that the two theater-goers are only this moment returned. Abigail is still in her opera cloak, and Harry leaning over the back of his mother's chair, in which she lies all white and muslin-clad. Her garment is a dainty hybrid between the homeliness of a bedroom dressing gown and the assumptions of a tea gown. She is lifting a small face of listening adoration to him. At the noise of the entering party both naturally look toward the door, and the hindmost of the invaders has not her view so obstructed by those who precede her as to miss the change of expression in both faces. The first emotion which the countenance of the woman whom she is so deeply desirous to propitiate exhibits, when turned upon her, is one of unmistakable dismay and disgust.

Clarence had fully meant to have related to his mother the fact of Miss Lisle's presence in St. Gratian—an intention the less meritorious on his part since, if he had not done so, Abigail would certainly have saved him the trouble. Even if there were no Abigail, bubbling over with admiring curiosity, Mrs. Clarence could not fail to discover it for herself in twenty-four hours.

He has established himself behind her chair with that very view, choosing that to some degree concealed position in order to utter his piece of news with a more natural and *dégagé* air. And now that thing which, of all others, he would most dislike and deprecate has happened.

Without being given any time to prepare her in any degree for the shock, he sees the introduction to his mother, which he would have prepared with so trembling a care, forced upon her at an untimely hour with unseemly brusqueness, and in the manner most of all certain to arouse her prejudices against the person so forced, or forcing herself, upon her acquaintance! How will his mother—already, as he divines her, more than ready to disapprove—conjecture the profound annoyance in the girl's heart, the deep mortification which he guesses, under the mask of her small, self-contained face? One thing he is spared; he does not suspect the extremely bitter drop which he himself contributes to his love's cup in that humiliating moment, and which flows from the look in his own face as she first catches sight of it above his mother's head—a look of dismay at least as profound as his parent's.

"Here is a surprise for you!" cries Lady Bramshill, coming in with a *frou-frou* of her ample skirts, and a total absence of misgiving as to her welcome-

ness, as, indeed, nothing would have pleased her
better than to have the same trick played upon herself. "There's nothing like the *imprévu*, is there?
The girls said that you would be in bed; but I knew
better. I remembered what a hopeless rake you
always were! Ha, ha!"

Mrs. Clarence has risen, and is holding out a
mechanical hand to the personified garrulity before
her. But her eyes have gone beyond her—beyond
Euphemia, beyond the bugled widow—and are resting
on the small and motionless figure standing just
within the door.

The two women who hold Clarence's life-strings
are looking at each other, and, with a sharp pang of
foreboding, he sees that on one side at least there is
no prepossession in the glance.

"You do not mind our taking you by storm?"
asks Lady Bramshill, for even in her the hostess'
manner is breeding a slight misgiving. "Of course,
it is most audacious of us; but what is the use of
having friends if one may not take liberties with
them that one cannot with mere acquaintances?
And if you do not want us, make no scruple of sending us away. The carriage will be here in a minute."

This suggestion, indicating a lack of cordiality in
her manner, brings Mrs. Clarence round:

"Oh, pray sit down!" she says, with a civility
whose formality rings ominously in her son's ears.
"I was a little startled at first. Will not these ladies
sit down?"

"I am forgetting my manners!" cries Lady
Bramshill, not yet quite reassured as to the wisdom

of her freak, and carrying it off, as her daughter feels, with a double portion of good-humor and bounce. "I must present you all to each other. This," indicating the elder lady, " is Mrs. Dynevor, with whom we lived and loved at Calcutta ; and this is Miss Lisle, who, I find, is an old acquaintance of Harry's. By the bye, Harry, what did you mean by not coming to speak to us at the play?" Then,. feeling that her question has fallen mysteriously flat, she goes on : "What delicious-looking sandwiches ! When first we came home from India, people asked us what were the changes that struck us most in England. The judge said the increase in the number of omnibuses ; and *I* said the improvement in sandwiches ! "

This rigmarole string of remarks arouses Mrs. Clarence to a sense of her duties, and she moves toward a table spread with slight cold foods, iced water, and a claret-jug. As she does so her pocket handkerchief slips, unperceived by her, to the floor, and Honor, who has been drawn forward to be presented, stoops, and, picking it up, restores it to her.

There seems to Harry a deprecating grace in the action—a touching indication of reverence and apology that must soften the flintiest heart.

No one can deny that there is also grace—since she can do nothing ungracefully—in Mrs. Clarence's mode of reception of the attention, faultless politeness in her thanks, and regrets at having given trouble. But if there is grace, there is—too perceptible to her son's anxious eyes and ears—frost, too. To Honor, since she sees his mother for the first time, the degree of chilliness or warmth of her ordinary manner must be unknown. But her senses have been rendered sharper than most people's by her outdoor life, and by her long habit of looking and listening in field and wood for the small noises and light movements of the lesser peoples of earth and air. It may be the quick sense of that chill which sends her back to her first position near the door.

All through the one-sided dialogue (a bull!) carried on between his mother and Lady Bramshill, Harry hears her few short, soft sentences dropped between the paragraphs of the widow's fluent comments on the night's entertainment and its heroine.

"Did you see that huge diamond sun which she wore on her corsage?" asks Mrs. Dynevor. "You know who gave it her? The Duke of ———, and they say that the diamonds were taken out of that historic *couronne fermée* of the duchess' which belonged to Catherine of Russia."

"Yes, I know that they say so."

"They were replaced by paste, but as the duchess does not know that, she no doubt wears her coronet quite as happily as before; but if ever she finds out, I would not be he."

"I should think that she despised him too much to care."

"H'm! no doubt, no doubt! So disgraceful in a man of his age, too! But, still, diamonds are always diamonds!"

"When everything else worth having in one's life had gone, I think the diamonds might go, too."

She says it in a very low voice, and with an accent

of concentrated scorn, yet, low as her voice is, he knows that his mother has heard the words. To him, and surely also to her, they come stamped with the seal of the girl's high-minded purity. Yet he would have been glad that the first specimen of his love's never very abounding talk which comes to his parent's ears should have been on a less dubious theme. He has presently cause to deepen and enlarge this wish.

"Well," says the widow, with a lenient laugh dedicated to the ducal follies, "he has more excuse for his weakness than men often have. Such coarse, ugly creatures befool them! but she is certainly extremely pretty and ladylike, so like a Greuze."

"She is not at all pretty off the stage."

"You have seen her off the stage?" with greatly heightened interest.

"Yes."

"And she is not really pretty?"

"When she speaks she is not at all pretty."

"Who is not at all pretty when she speaks?" asks Lady Bramshill, beginning to discern the extremely intermittent nature of the attention which Mrs. Clarence is giving to her own converse.

"Poppy de Vere," replies the widow; "but"—incredulously—"I can scarcely believe it. Who told you so?"

"I have spoken to her."

"You have spoken to her? *spoken to Poppy de Vere?*"

"She stayed at my father's house. Her husband is a racing friend of my father's."

The widow's jaw drops. She is not acquainted

with Honor's history, and the calmness with which she proclaims an acquaintance with the too illustrious Poppy strikes her for an instant silent. But only for an instant. A fire of eager questions follows:

"Is she nice? At least, not nice, really, of course—at all refined, I mean? or like a lady? Would you ever guess?"

"She is not at all nice. She sits with her feet on the chimneypiece. She swears a good deal. It would be impossible for anyone to be less nice."

"But why on earth"—astonishment getting the upper hand of good manners in this searching query—"did you consent to meet her? Why did not you go away?"

"I did not know that she was coming; but if I had I should not have gone away. My father would have been displeased, and she did not do me any harm."

She says it with the quietude of complete conviction, and then there is a pause. The other dialogues, having for some minutes paid their tribute to the superior interest of this one by perceptible slackening, are now dropped into silence. It is broken only by an inaudible—save to her son and the person addressed—murmur from Mrs. Clarence to Abigail, which Harry knows to be a suggestion to his young cousin to go to bed. He knows, too, that the suggestion has been dictated by the feeling that the conversation of his heart's high pure lady is not fit for her to listen to. The conviction is an inexpressibly bitter one.

Abigail steals reluctantly away, and ten more heavy,

flat minutes follow before the welcome sound of wheels on the pavement outside announces that deliverance has come. Deliverance? Yes. But yet it is a salvation that, if the young man do not make some effort to prevent it, will involve his letting his love pass from under his churlish roof without one word of the reverent, glad welcome which, if Fate had not played him so scurvy a trick as to the manner of her coming, he would have offered her. Even if his mother perceive the manœuver by which his end is gained, he must make himself elbow and voice room for one little word to her.

The opportunity he seeks comes quite naturally after all. For just two minutes they stand on the doorstep together and alone. But with the come opportunity, the power goes. What can he say in the meager space that will be his, good enough, respectful enough, tender enough, to remove the cold and bitter impression which she must be taking away with her from his home? While he hesitates, a minute and a half of the two minutes go by. And she does not help him. She has suffered far more than he: suffered in her maidenly dignity, in her self-respect; and though her face keeps its trained grave sweetness, without any trace of resentment, yet she cannot quite compass speech. And she is never a great talker.

Lady Bramshill's heavy foot—she had gone back for one of those last words, of which, unlike Honor, she has always such a copious stock—is heard in the little hall close behind them.

There is only half a moment left. And yet into

half a minute many a pregnant sentence that has altered the whole lie of a life has been packed ere now. His tardy utterance, when it comes, can hardly have that effect.

"What a very fine night!"

"Yes; but the farmers are crying out for rain."

And she is gone. He returns to the smoking room profoundly dissatisfied, but with a heart that, under its disgusted ache, has yet a leap in it. He finds his mother standing, with her back turned toward him, leaning against the lintel of the French window, which, so suave is the breath of the lovely summer night, still stands wide open. Her head is propped against the wall, and there is dejection in the very hang of her diaphanous draperies. He possesses himself softly of one of her limply pendent hands.

"You will catch cold."

"I do not think so."

A little pause. He had rather that she should be the one to begin the subject; but since she will not, the power of self-control being suddenly withdrawn from him, he must himself rush into it. He does it by the monosyllable "Well?" Only a monosyllable, yet so full of passionate expectation that her heart stands still. She knows that one of the opportunities of her life has come—one of those opportunities that, if we once let slip, we can never, so swiftly do they run, overtake.

"Well, dear?" the vague returning of his own word upon him is, as she knows, only a putting off the evil day.

"Do you—do you see the likeness that I have told you of?"

Perhaps if he had worded his bid for admiration differently, she might have been better able to rise to it. But against his demand thus made her whole being rises in unconquerable revolt. It is herself, then, who is to be made the instrument of her murder.

"Miss Lisle and I are both little pale black women," she answers, in a very, very small voice. "I do not think that I see any other likeness."

There is a pause. He has dropped her hand and turned away, and she knows that she has let her priceless opportunity go, and that, at one of the most crucial points of her life's road, she has taken the wrong turning.

She knows it better still next morning, when, soon after breakfast, she sees him set off in riding-breeches, and with his whip under his arm, toward the stables where he keeps his horse. He had come down late to breakfast, when Abigail and she had all but finished that repast, which, in Mrs. Clarence's case, on this occasion, is a mere form, and he had begged them not to wait for him, so that she has scarcely exchanged words with him.

She had meant to have taken some step—even a whole sleepless night had not suggested to her its exact nature—toward repairing her false move, and now it is too late. He has gone unpropitiated, full of resentment and wounded feeling, to have balm poured on his hurts by that hand which, had she been wise, she would have controlled herself into taking into her own.

"How early he is going out riding to-day!" cries Abigail, from her window post. "What a nice flat back he has, and how well his legs look in those gaiters! Quite a poem!"—laughing—"as that Miss Lisle said about Poppy de Vere's."

"*Miss Lisle said so?*" in an extremely shocked voice. "I do not think that it was Miss Lisle; it was the other lady—the jetty one."

But, despite this almost confident rehabilitation of poor Honor, Mrs. Clarence keeps a silent inward conviction that the silly and objectionable remark made had issued from Miss Lisle's lips. What an abyss it opens between herself and the girl who could be supposed capable of uttering it! She lapses into a silence, whose distress is heightened by this tiny incident, which, so little do we gauge the force of our own light words, passes so entirely from Abigail's mind that her next remark is a wish that the Vaughans would let in their dog, as "he has been waiting at the door for ages," coupled with the observation that "the footman and he are evidently great friends, but that he is afraid of the housemaid!"

CHAPTER X.

MEANWHILE, trotting along the green grass margin of the white highroad, cutting across pasture lands, and skirting hay-meadows, Clarence is making but a brief thing of the interval between the dowdy, semi-animate little town and the newly painted and smartened-up and generally alive and teeming country house which is his goal. He reaches it only just in time, for as he comes in sight of the hall door he sees three just mounted people in the act, or hovering on the verge of the act, of setting forth on a ride.

The lateness of the young brother who is to escort the two girls, which Clarence learns from the hang-dog air of the culprit under a rather needlessly austere rebuke from his sister, is the only reason why he has not missed the party altogether, since they would have taken a road different from that by which he had approached. Although he has lacked Miss Lisle's society for all but one week of his life without any very perceptible consequent diminution of flesh and appetite, yet to have lost this one more morning seems to him, now that he has just escaped doing so, a calamity greater than he could have borne.

Her face is at first almost hidden from him, stooping toward a large white terrier, which he recognizes as Adolphus' Nipper, and which is standing up on hind legs against the leg of the horse, evidently requesting to be taken up. That such a request should be complied with would, under the circumstances, have never occurred to the young man, and it is with stupefaction that he now sees him lifted by a groom and placed under Miss Lisle's arm.

"Why do you carry him?" he asks, going quickly round to her; and this natural question solves the difficulty of how to open a conversation in which the *contretemps* of last night must be fresh in both minds. "Why do you carry him? He is perfectly well able to run."

"I know that he is; he likes running with horses or a carriage."

"Then why do you carry him?"

"He is rather an eccentric character," she answers, breaking into one of her slight grave smiles, "and he declines to come at all unless he is carried for the first hundred yards. And one would not"—with an affectionate pressure of her elbow against his side—"lose the pleasure of his company for such a trifle."

"I have tried to persuade Miss Lisle," says Euphemia, putting her horse in motion, "to let me at least take turns in carrying him. No one can imagine how disagreeable it is until they have tried it; and he *moults* so much that he covers one with white hairs."

"It is all the more reason why he should not cover *two*," replies Honor quietly.

The young man involuntarily turns his head over his shoulder as she speaks. He has had no invitation to join the party, but as he has on several previous occasions ridden with members of the Bramshill family, it seems taken for granted that he should do so now.

"We have been rather alarmed of late by signs of a new development of Nipper's tyranny," says Euphemia: "an inclination to refuse to set off even on a walk without being carried for his usual hundred yards."

"I should resist that," replies Clarence. "He is young and strong, and has no excuse of age or delicacy."

But he is not thinking of what he is saying. He is thinking of the "neat excellence" with which that backward glance had shown him that the feat of carrying a large dog under her bridle-arm by a young lady on a horse inclined to be fidgety may be performed. He is thinking, too, of how an alteration in the order of their going may be effected without a too perceptible maneuver on his part.

A kindly gate with an obstructive fastening gives him the opportunity he desires; for Miss Lisle, growing tired of the long fumbling, puts her horse at the low fence which skirts the field into which they are seeking entrance, and Harry thinks himself justified in following her. Euphemia, who, like many large and domineering personalities, is a timid horsewoman, declines to follow suit; so the other two—Honor having happily rid herself of her incumbrance before her jump—ride slowly on.

Clarence has secured the *tête-à-tête* he has coveted, but for the first few moments he seems incapable of making any use of it. They have crossed a little pasture, and entered a wood, before he is delivered of the not very pregnant remark :

"There is quite as much variety in the character of dogs as in that of people."

"Quite."

There is nothing abrupt or intentionally *shutting up* in the monosyllable, but it does not lead to anything. Is there—or is it his guilty fancy?—a slight shade of reticent dignity in his companion's manner which differentiates it from her Eastshire one, quiet as that was? An allusion to last night will perhaps clear up the self-put question.

"You got home all right last night?"

A sprightlier-minded person than Miss Lisle might well have inquired whether, had she *not* got home all right, she would be likely to be now riding by his side through the wood's green light.

But Honor is not sprightly. She merely replies: "Quite right, thank you;" and again there seems a brick wall at the end of the sentence.

But if there is, it is, to his surprise, she who over-climbs it.

"After having seen us together, do you still think I am like—Mrs. Clarence?"

She does not look at him as she puts the question, which might, indeed, seem to challenge an examination of her features, and she hesitates before the last two words, as if in doubt whether to say "your mother" or "Mrs. Clarence."

That she ends by choosing the more formal title proves to the young man that she is aware of her own overnight failure to recommend herself to his parent.

"I think it even more startling"—emphatically.

She is so little in the habit of showing emotion, that he dares hardly believe that he detects, by a deepened dimple in the only cheek that he can speculate upon, that his answer gives her pleasure.

"And did she herself see it? Have you ever suggested it to her?"

An almost imperceptible sinking of the voice alone reveals that the answer to this question is of any import to the speaker. He knows that she sees the lame unreadiness of his response.

"People—don't you think?—very seldom know what they themselves are like. She sees it to a certain extent, but not to the degree that I do."

He has no indication as to whether the reply disappoints her, since at the moment she is now warding off from her quite averted face with her whip handle an arching briar branch, rough with swelling rosebuds, which is threatening to sweep across her.

When she does speak, it is in a tone of composed but evidently heartfelt admiration.

"She is a very beautiful lady!"

The deep respect and profound appreciation evidenced by both the phrase and the tone that carries it make flash back on his memory by contrast the slightingness of his mother's words: "Miss Lisle and I are both little pale black women. I do not think I see much other likeness"—words in which the depreciation is not the less thorough because she has coupled herself with the person *dénigrée*. We have all in our day practiced this subtle mode of aspersion.

For the first time in his life he compares his mother in his mind *un*favorably with another woman.

Even if that mother's verdict upon Honor had been as flattering as the girl's upon her, the reverential courtesy toward all women in which he has been from infancy bred, and which comes doubly easy to him in the case of the woman he loves, would prevent his telling her so to her face. Yet to his vicariously guilty conscience—guilty, that is, of another's offense—it seems that the silence which follows her remark must appear to her an ominous one. He can only answer it by a grateful look, whose quality she very probably does not recognize.

They pass on in silence through the sunshot green tangle, where the ride is here and there so overflung, overgrown by encroaching undergrowth, that they have to pass along in single file.

He has come up with her again, after one such short separation, to find by the serenity of her bright face how entirely any little mortification, if it ever existed, has been shone and sung out to her. He remembers her having once told him that she never could be very unhappy out of doors. Her chin is a little lifted, and her lips apart to drink in the filtered radiance, and her pretty ears are cocked to disentangle the talk of the birds—to him, as to most of us, a pleasing but unintelligible babel; to her the conversation of intimate and well-understood friends.

"Do you hear the wood wren?" she asks.

"I have no doubt that I do,"—laughing—"but I could not put a name to it."

"Oh, yes, you could. It says *Please! please!* as if begging you to go away."

"Does it?"

"It has two notes. The first is a tick, tick, tick, with a long p-r-r-r-h at the end. There! do not you hear him? You cannot mistake him."

"Cannot I?"

"There is a tom-tit imitating a chiff-chaff."

He pulls up his horse and strains his ears, but is quite unable to pick out of the melodious jumble about and above him the tiny mimicry alluded to.

"It is so odd that you cannot hear it!" she says, with a smile of unaffected surprise; then, afraid of having been discourteous, hastens to add: "I always think your hearing so very acute. But it is all a matter of habit; and the way in which birds imitate one another is very puzzling. It was a long time before I found out that thrushes imitate owls."

"*Do* they?"

"Yes; not accurately, of course, but still cleverly. I always wonder if they recognize their own language when it is so garbled."

"They probably feel like a Frenchman when an Englishman addresses him in dog French."

"It was so odd at first to see parrots flying about in India. We spent Christmas Day among the ruins of Old Delhi. There is a wonderful ancient tower there—but no doubt you know that—which they call the Kootub, and which Mrs. Bevis wanted to see; and we took our luncheon, and ate it among those miles of ruins; and the green parrots flew overhead, and the little squirrels rustled and played."

She pauses, with a look of recollected enjoyment. It is an unusually long speech for her; and her hearer takes her communicativeness thankfully, as a sign of renewed or reviving intimacy.

"You liked your India, didn't you?"

"Ye-es."

"That sounds a little doubtful."

"I liked the jungle; I liked all the *out*door part. You know I always hate temples and sights and ruins."

He feels a momentary jar. Memory shows him in a flash a contrasting picture of his mother as a travelling companion—her acute and cultivated interest in all that foreign travel can show. A few minutes ago a mental comparison had set her at a disadvantage, now the balance is redressed.

"I felt my ignorance rather oppressively all the time that I was there."

He draws a long breath, disarmed and reconciled to the barbarism of her first utterance by the—as he feels—regretful humility of her second.

"More than you do in England?" in a tone of delicate sympathy, not attempting to deny the fact, which, indeed, seeing his acquaintance with the furniture of his companion's mind, would be flattery too patent, but trying to convey a soothing implication that the evil is not an irremediable one.

"I do not feel it at all in England," replies she composedly; "at least"—with a tiny grain of malice—"I did not until you took such pains to rub it well into me last year in Eastshire."

Again he feels a slight sense of disappointment.

He had hoped at their last meeting that he had raised a piquant curiosity in her slumbering intelligence— slumbering only for books, so awake and alert in other directions.

"I suppose it was the contrast with Mrs. Bevis that did it," pursues she reflectively. "I cannot think how she can have borne my company. She had taken lessons in Hindustanee, and read three lives of Buddha and two histories of India. She had everything about every conqueror of India, from Bacchus—had not he something to say to India, or have I got the wrong end of the stick there, too?—to Lord Clive, at her fingers' ends."

"She is a very intelligent woman."

Before it is quite uttered he knows that there is something at once trite and snubbing in the shape of the sentence, and yet enough vexation lingers in his system to prevent his arresting its utterance.

But the shaft glances harmless from Honor's armor.

"Yes; isn't she?" replies she warmly. "I was always being struck afresh with it. She knew all about every single place we visited. And it did not give me the impression that she had crammed, either; it all came so naturally."

He does not know what possesses him, but the preaching instinct still seems to drive him.

"And it gave you an impulse to go and do likewise?"

He speaks with a smile, but he himself knows it to be of a governessy quality.

She looks meditatively in front of her, straight between her horse's ears.

"I do not think it did, in the least."

There is a pause, his delight in her—he seems to himself to have forgotten of how acute a quality it was—again slightly rubbed.

"Are you aware that you are contradicting yourself?" he asks half playfully, and yet with a sublying seriousness. "Five minutes ago you told me that you had been oppressed by the sense of your own ignorance."

She shows no sign of discomfiture at this confrontation with her own utterance.

"One may be oppressed by a thing without feeling the slightest impulse to change it, because one knows it would be perfectly hopeless. I was never any hand at book-learning when I was a child, and I do not think I am likely to begin now."

Against so resolved a profession of ignorance he feels that his weapons would be vain, and he receives it in silence.

Composed as she looks, his muteness may fidget her, for she presently resumes :

"I think that there must be other people like me ; but if not, I cannot help it—I am made like that."

"Yes?"

"I like, I always have liked, and I always shall like, the things that one can admire and love without any education at all—that one has not to pump up one's appreciation for out of histories and catalogues and biographies. I like all the *out*side things. You must remember"—with a slight beam of triumph at this clinching argument—"it was God who made *them*, and he did not make the others."

"No?"

"Now, what education"—the victorious beam browing brighter—"does it require to enjoy *that?*"

She has pulled up her horse as she speaks, and is pointing with her hunting crop down a glade in the wood whose mouth they have reached with the end of her sentence. It is a long narrow vista, at the present moment lilac-flushed on either side by rhododendrons in full bloom. On their various-shaded flower masses the flecking sunshine is playing through the young oak trees above them.

"And yet it is only an educated eye that would much care for it."

But he says it slackly, his tutoring impulse swallowed up and dissolved in pleasure.

She is apparently no stickler for having the last word, as she makes no rejoinder, and it is not till their horses are once again in motion that she next speaks—not with any great fluency even then:

"I suppose that your mother—Mrs. Clarence—is extremely cultivated. That is the right phrase, isn't it?"

"*Cultivated!*" he repeats thoughtfully. "Well, no, I should not call her that. She is no great reader—except of books of devotion."

"I suppose that she is a sort of saint"—a little under her breath.

He does not answer, except by a smile of such reverent tenderness as gives the heart of the girl beside him a slight twinge of vague pain. But that heart is too generous to entertain so unworthy a guest for a second longer than she is conscious of its presence. If she were to die for it, she would never be able to summon such a look as that which it has just worn to her companion's face. But that is *her* fault, not his.

"My mother has wonderfully true and fine instincts about art and literature. She does not, as you announced that *you* did the first time I had the pleasure of meeting you, think reading 'such waste of time.'"

He is smiling, but the quality of his smile has entirely changed.

"I am afraid that I still think so," rejoins she, with a gentle, hopeless steadfastness that makes him laugh—"at least, I think it so as far as I personally am concerned. Do you remember what pains you took to enlighten my darkness last year in Eastshire?"

"And you are going to have the heart to tell me that all my labor was wasted?"

"I am afraid so," very gravely and contritely, but quite firmly. "Not that I did not make an effort; for after you left I tried conscientiously to read some of the books you had recommended to me, and I did get through two or three of them."

"*Get through!*"

"Well, I assure you that to me it was *get through*, which, I suppose, is the measure of my hopelessness."

Again he laughs, but a little ruefully.

"I got on best with one of Browning's."

"Browning?" hopefully and surprisedly.

"It was 'How They Brought the Good News from——.'"

She pauses.

"Now, where was it that they brought it from? I did not mind that one much, only I never found out what the good news was; and Mrs. Bevis was rather vexed with me for saying that what struck me most in the poem was the disgraceful way in which they treated their horses. It was almost as brutal as the military ride from Berlin to Vienna."

"Not quite"—smiling. "'Dirk and Joris and I' had at least more excuse. And that was your greatest achievement?"

"Yes; I stuck fast in all the others. But then the weather was extremely fine, and we had to break in the filly? Do you remember the filly? Well, she is going to make a first-rate tandem-leader."

Her voice is not more raised than when recounting her literary disasters, but the tone of warm enthusiasm that runs through it contrasts racily with the flat lugubriousness of her preceding confessions, and he laughs. But even while laughing the thought flashes thankfully across him that his mother is not within earshot.

It must be the result of the freemasonry we often find existing between our brains that Honor's next observation shows that Mrs. Clarence had got into her thoughts at the same instant as she had stepped into her son's.

"Mrs. Clarence does not ride?"

"I have no reason for supposing that she ever was in the saddle in her life."

"She does not know or care anything at all about horses, I dare say?"

"You would think her culpably ignorant."

"And in everything else *she* would think *me* culpably ignorant!"

This is so perfectly true that his only resource is to answer, in jocose assent :

"Culpably."

But, seeing or fancying that her face falls, he adds seriously, and, as he feels, a little pedantically :

"My mother never judges anyone harshly."

"Not even *us*, when we broke in upon her last night?"

He notices that she never looks at him when she puts questions to him about his mother.

"Why do you ask that?" with a precipitation which he feels is in itself an answer to her question. "She was taken by surprise. She is a very shy woman, and lives very much out of the world. You must not attach importance to any indications of— of—dism—of surprise that she showed."

They have left the wood, and entered a lane scarcely less vocal than the woodland they have quitted. A thrush close to them is singing on a bough, voluble one moment, silent the next, listening apparently to a lark, faint with distance—a lark playing its little instrument with muted strings.

He would fain hope that it is her listening to the music that keeps her silent, not unfaith in his crippled apology. But her next remark knocks this walking-stick out of his hand.

"I am going to ask you a perfectly unjustifiable question, and you are, of course, quite at liberty to disregard it." Again her gaze is directed between her horse's ears to a village spire at the lane end. "Did I last night—did I do or say anything likely to provoke Mrs. Clarence's disapproval?"

Her question fills him with astonished dismay, and he sees the tell-tale nature of his tardiness to respond in the slow, deep stain stealing over the one cheek he can see.

"I—I do not think I quite understand. Why, you hardly spoke!"

"It is egotistical of me to suppose that she noticed me at all; but I had an instinct that she took a dislike to me."

There is another betraying pause. He knows that to her transparent and almost brutal truthfulness—the truthfulness of the savage and the dog—evasion will be vain, and will only degrade him in her eyes. Yet how tear open, widen into a chasm, the little rift he already grievingly sees existing between the two soverigns of his heart, by owning that his love's eyes, keen with watching nature's obscure and silent processes—keen for all their softness—have divined aright?

He takes shelter—a poor tumble-down, unweathertight shelter—in a generality:

"Don't you think it is a mistake to conclude on insufficient evidence that people dislike you?"

"I am quite aware that it is a form of conceit to imagine that strangers occupy themselves at all about one; and if you tell me that I am mistaken, I will believe you."

As she speaks, she removes her eyes from the distant steeple, and, contrary to what has been her habit throughout the ride, places them upon his. The action removes his last chance of vamping up a successful lie. He makes the best of a bad job.

"I will tell you the exact truth. My mother has got a wrong conception of you."

"How?"

The brief directness of this question throws him once again on his beam-ends. She waits a second and then adds quietly :

"I do not quite see how she can have any conception of me at all except from what you may have told her of me—if you have happened to mention me."

"You are quite right. It is that I have given it to her"—in a tone of acute vexation.

At the look of wonder, a little tinged with gentle reproach, that comes into the eyes which are still meeting his, he loses his hesitancy.

"When I came back from Eastshire I was naturally very full of my visit. The life had been so new to me—its unconventionality, its out-of-doorness, and yet its intellectual element."

"Yes, it is a nice life."

"I told her of your 'leading' in the harvest field; of your sailing the boat, and breaking in the filly; of your shrimping; of your varied activities, in fact."

"Yes?"

"You know what things *words* are—what clumsy contrivances for misleading. I need not tell you that that was not the impression I intended to convey; but I fear she gathered the idea that you must be rather—masculine!"

Evidently she is not going to be hasty in commenting on his blundering.

"I am not masculine-looking," she says at last, in that tone of firm and quiet self-respect—in naught akin to vanity—which he had learned last year from Mrs. Bevis to be the outcome of her difficult and thorny life.

He knows that her implication is that one look at her must have removed the impression of her mannishness. He repeats the word after her, as if only so could he convey the strength of his repudiation of the epithet. Then, afraid that the emphasis of his tone may have scared her—and, indeed, it has had the effect of making her at once wincingly turn away her head, he hurries on:

"The misconception is, of course, ludicrous. One glance would suffice to prove that."

"Then why, having seen me, did Mrs. Clarence still think me masculine?"

"She did not think you masculine,"—lamely eating his words,—" but——"

"But what?"

He is silent, and it is she who, still quite quietly, but with a risen color, resumes:

"Did I say anything likely to confirm that impression? I do not quite remember, but I think I said very little. Other people were talking; there was no need of me."

Still silence.

"I cannot recall what was the subject of conversation"—drawing her brows together. "Let me see. Oh, yes! Mrs. Dynevor was asking me about Poppy de Vere."

She has given him his lead, and loosened the string of his tongue. It is not very loose even now.

"I know you will not misunderstand me—I am sure you will comprehend"—floundering—"how little intention—— The fact is, that my mother—she herself always says that she is quite a hundred years behind the time—may have been a little—a little—surprised at your having any information to give on such a topic."

It seems to himself an odious sentence the moment it is out of his mouth. He dares not look to see how she takes it.

It is a long minute before she answers, in a tone that he has not yet heard :

"I should have been rather stupid if I had not had information to give about her when I had stayed a week in the house with her."

"A week?"

"Yes. She and Lord Camelot came for a race-week."

"And you went to the races with them?"

"No. My father did not insist on my going, so I stayed at home. But if I *had* gone, I should not have been at all afraid of Poppy de Vere doing *me* any harm."

There is a ring of indescribable pride and self-reliance in her voice, through which he yet feels that a strain of bitter mortification pierces.

He casts a remorseful glance at her. She is sitting dart upright, and her head is held high, but she looks a very small, slight thing to carry such a bold front against a destiny so unjustly ugly.

"I am sure that no one would admire your courage more than my mother," he says, trying futilely to repair the mischief he has done, and succeeding, as he is stingingly conscious, only in being flat and lying. "But her ignorance of the world amounts to a positive misfortune. Her mind is the most extraordinarily innocent one I have ever come into contact with!"

He breaks off, with a suspicion that he is conveying the impression that his hearer's mind is not an innocent one, but, as she does not help him, goes on presently:

"She has lived so much out of the world, has kept such an astounding ignorance of evil, that when the existence of it is forced upon her it makes her really *ill!*"

"She is a very fortunate lady," replies the girl dryly, yet sadly too. "No wonder that she did not like me!"

And Clarence feels that his effort to pave the way for a reciprocal admiration between his two beloved women, by insuring himself against the danger of his love's a second time airing her knowledge of the *demi-monde* to his parent, has resulted only in deepening by several fathoms the rift he had sought to close.

CHAPTER XI.

The Bramshill's are apparently in no hurry to return to the expensive London house which they have taken for the season. Perhaps their experience of it between Easter and Whitsun has shown them the not altogether new fact that you may be a very significant person on the banks of the Hooghly, and a very insignificant one on the banks of the Thames. Perhaps Euphemia's family have made the discovery that there are too many seven feet of young female stature, too many miraculous roseleaf skins, in Hyde Park for any one such to take the town by storm. Perhaps—the most charitable supposition—Euphemia herself prefers the cool nightingales and lilacs, the golf and croquet, of The Beeches to the hotter and more heart-burning joys of London. And Honor stays on with her.

There is nothing surprising in the fact of a sister-less girl desiring to prolong a companionship which an accidental meeting in a London street had renewed, and which both have found congenial. Yet the day on which Lady Bramshill has announced, in the tone of one giving a piece of good news, " Honor is going to stay on with us—no, not for another week ; do not interrupt, child !" with a shaken fore-finger as she attempts to slide in a limitation ; "but indefinitely," is one that is marked in Mrs. Clarence's history by a longer kneeling in her little improvised oratory, by blacker-rimmed eyes, and a fainter voice than on any previous occasion.

The smallness of his mother's voice, on which he had been wont to rally her, has got of late upon Harry's nerves. He does not give himself the opportunity of being exposed to its irritation for long together, both because the courts have resumed their sittings, and because what leisure his attendance upon them leaves him is spent under another roof than hers. It is spent chiefly under no roof at all: for whoever would court Honor Lisle must do it under the cope of heaven.

And that he is courting Honor Lisle is a fact that he no longer tries to conceal from himself. Of the two mastering influences of his life, the elder and weaker has gone to the wall. But that it has done so is, as he tells himself, its own fault. It is his mother's injustice to the woman he loves that has given the necessary impetus to his decision. As the days go by he sees how little nearer grows the *rapprochement* he had hoped for between them—the *rapprochement* that he had imagined needed only a better knowledge to bloom into fullest appreciation, and for which one at least had been so ready, till his own clumsy hand warned her off.

They have met but seldom and always accidentally, as Mrs. Clarence has not once visited The Beeches since Miss Lisle's arrival—an ommission which in his heart he resents, though it is, in fact, but the continuation of a habit of abstinence ; nor has Honor once again accompanied Lady Bramshill in one of her not infrequent raids upon the little house in St. Gratian. Once or twice they have met in the street.

The subject forever not only uppermost in, but solely occupying, the hearts and minds of mother and son is now never mentioned between them. Since they do not talk of that, there seems to be nothing else in the whole range of creation to talk about. Their conversation, once so free and full, has dwindled to a thread, and they both—or he thinks so—avoid possibilities of a *tête-à-tête*.

Once or twice the now draggingness of her step, the languor of her eyes, and her flagging appetite, drive a needle of pain into him; but he steels himself against her with the reflection of how little real love for himself her mute and sullen resistance to his attainment of what she knows to be the one thing he has ever passionately wished argues.

Her perpetual church-going frets him. He does not know with what an agony of ache she sees the slackening of his little daily kindnesses, nor that it is in deadly fight with the tortures of jealous hatred that are wringing her being that she kneels for such endless hours in the church of whose draughtiness he so carpingly reminds her.

One day she emerges from the porch partially victorious.

"Why does your Miss Lisle never come here?" she asks, when next she meets her son—says it with an abruptness not like her, and arguing a fear of not being able to put the question if she risk keeping it long by her.

The light and warmth which seem to her to have

been so long absent from his eyes, when turned upon her, spring back into them.

"Would you like her to come?"

"I do not want to force her inclinations"—with a little pallid smile, that yet tries hard to be cordial—"but, if she is willing——"

"There can be no doubt of *that!*" puts in Abigail, who has just, to Harry's annoyance, entered the room, and speaking with officious goodwill.

"Has she ever—I mean have you any reason for supposing—has she ever expressed a wish?"

"No-o, not exactly; but, being such a friend of Harry's of course she *must* want you to like her!"

The mother catches her breath, and the son, inwardly cursing the clumsiness of his ally, hastens to take up his own parable; but his touch is scarcely lighter or more fortunate than his cousin's.

"What day would you like to see her? When shall I bring her?"

If it had been his object to choose the most unfortunate verb that he could light on, he could not have been more successful. *Bring!* What an implication of command over Miss Lisle's actions and intentions it carries in its very sound! But Mrs. Clarence's heroism still lasts.

"You know that I am not very apt to be out. I should wish her to suit her own convenience."

The words are stiff, and the tone is faint and dry; but he is too much overjoyed at the unlooked-for overture to pry too nicely into details.

"Her convenience shall be yours!" he cries triumphantly; and again her ear is grated, this time by the *shall*.

He does not, or will not, perceive her silence, but once again takes up his old position at her feet, with his head laid on her knees.

"How *can* I thank you enough, my mother!" he sighs, almost under his breath.

The attitude is the old one, adopted in earliest childhood, and never since abandoned; but the integral difference in the spirit, coupled with the unveiled confession in his words, are too much for her. She spoils all—spoils it even while her hand is mechanically passing, with the familiar gesture of years, over his hair.

"You had better not thank me till the interview is over," she says, with a small quivering laugh. "You must be sure to be present, and to tell me what to talk about. I am afraid that your friend and I are not likely to have many topics in common. Do you know that, till she told us about her, I had never even heard of Poppy de Vere!"

This speech (Abigail had left the room immediately after her own unlucky utterance, either because she had only come in to fetch something, or warned away by the glare in her usually friendly cousin's eyes) this speech sends him off—it is one of his free afternoons—an hour earlier than he had intended to The Beeches.

That is, perhaps, the reason why he finds Euphemia sole occupant of the little habitual camp round the hammock in which she is lying.

"She will be back directly," says the young lady,

answering his look of balked expectation in a manner which shows how little deception as to the object of his search there is in her mind. "She is only strolling about somewhere. I think she does not want me to see how upset she is."

"Upset! By what?"

"By having to leave us to-morrow."

"*To-morrow!*"

"Yes, to-morrow. That unqualifiable father of hers has wired for her to come home at once, to entertain a party of blacklegs and Poppy de Veres for some steeplechases."

He is quite silent. She is going to-morrow; and, despite the implication in the verb *bring*, which had carried ice to his mother's heart, he has as yet no hold upon her—no assurance that this sudden slipping out of life may not be a final one.

He is roused by a laugh from Euphemia.

"Mother is signaling madly to us to come in to tea. I wonder what mischief she thinks we are hatching."

She says it with an air of deep amusement. The misconception into which Lady Bramshill had originally fallen, and which has been carefully fostered by her daughter for the sake of the amusement that her parent's distressed antics have afforded her, has also been nursed by Clarence. He knows instinctively that, had his hostess realized the lie of the land, she would not have been above rallying him upon it—a possibility at which his spirit shivers.

Miss Bramshill pauses a minute or two before obeying her mother's summons—knowing that she is watching her from the window—to bend her tall head languishingly toward the young man; but, though generally a willing enough confederate, he is now too preoccupied to take any part in her game, and they cross the sward in silence.

"You have heard our bad news?" says Lady Bramshill, greeting the young man with something less than her usual expansiveness. "We are going to lose our dear little Honor!" In a cheerfuller key: "We must have her here again next year."

Next year! What an infinite distance is conveyed by the promissory words!

"I never can remember whether you like milk or cream in your tea," pursued his hostess, adding placidly: "Adolphus will be inconsolable."

Since her mother's eyes are bent upon the teacups, Euphemia thinks that she may indulge herself in a smile of meaning amusement, thrown at Clarence across the table; but Lady Bramshill unluckily looks up at the moment. The discovery of the eyebeams being flung right under her very nose agitates her so much that she drops the sugar-tongs. Clarence stoops to pick them up; but, in the act of restoring them, pauses, arrested by the sight of a great fir bough entering at one of the French windows.

It is a moment before he realizes that the little figure carrying, and all but hidden by it, is that of the lady of his thoughts.

"I hope you will not mind," comes her small voice through its somber screen, "but I found a golden-crested wren's nest, and I thought Adolphus might like to see it."

At the end of her sentence there comes a slight change and catch in her voice, and her lover knows that she has seen him. They gather round and admire the houselet, cunningly hung to elude the passer's sight beneath the branch of a Douglas fir. It hangs just at the end of it, with pine needles and little twigs woven in to hold it up and make it secure. What a sweet little elfin home under the shower of enduring green, dark above and silvery below! How vivid and bright the fresh shoots of the pine!

Clarence helps its captor to hang it in trophy upon the rod of one of the electric lights in the hall. A golden-crested wren and the electric light! But the wrenlings had wisely flown before such a desecration of their woodland birthplace had happened.

Their joint occupation has a little isolated the couple from the other two, but not so much so but that Lady Bramshill's friendly plaint comes to their ears.

"It is a sweetly pretty thing, and it was exceedingly clever of you to find it; but I rather grudge your hunt for it, as it has robbed us of a bit of your company on your last day."

"*Your last day!*" repeats Clarence, in a voice warranted not to carry into the next room. "Why is it your last day?"

"Have you not heard? My father has sent for me."

"To another rendezvous with Poppy de Vere?"

The young man is as well aware as you or I that it is not good manners to fleer at a person to his nearest of kin, but his boiling indignation forces out the gibe. Her matter-of-fact answer shows neither resentment nor approbation:

"I do not know; he did not say."

"Why do you go?"

"Because my father tells me."

She repeats the answer with no sign of impatience; then, since wrath and sorrow keep him dumb, adds:

"Would *you* think it right to run exactly counter to your mother's wishes?"

There is, or he fancies it, an underlying meaning in her question, and it is to that underlying meaning that his answer is made.

"Yes," he says slowly and weightily; "there are conditions—circumstances under which I should undoubtedly think it my duty to run counter to her wishes; and whether it were my duty or not, I should do it."

The cool slowness of his beginning is exchanged in the latter half of his sentence for a pregnant hurry, and it seems to himself, when he has finished it, as if he had made a declaration. It appears to be the only chance of making one that will be given him.

Contrary to her usual custom, Lady Bramshill shows no inclination to leave the young people. She has generally seen them stroll away in a trio or quartet without showing any wish to join them. To-day their adjournment to the encampment round the hammock is made in her company, and when they try to stroll away she calls them back.

It has always been their custom to wander off in a band, and not separate till out of sight. But to-day all Clarence's efforts to abstract Honor from the rest of the party are vain. For some reason she will not connive at his attempts in that direction. They sit round, all either out of spirits or out of temper. Presently Euphemia picks up a book lying on the grass.

"Who has left his literature behind him? Poetry? It must be Adolphus' tutor; he is always imbibing poetry. I shall read aloud, to improve all our minds," adding, in a hastily snatched aside to Clarence, apropos of her parent, "She will never stand it; it will drive her away."

She begins in a drawling voice:

"It was the frog in the well—
Humbledum, thumbledum;
And the merry mouse in the mill—
Tweedle, tweedle, twino.

"The frog would a-wooing ride,
Sword and buckler by his side.

"When he upon his high horse set,
His boots they shone as black as jet.

"When he came to the merry mill-pin—
'Lady mouse, live you within?'

"Then came out the dusty mouse:
'I am lady of this house.

"'Hast thou any mind of me?'
'I have e'en great mind of thee.'"

There is a sound of shuffling on one of the garden chairs.

"What fearful rubbish!" says Lady Bramshill, a streak of pettishness in her good-humored voice.

"Come and tell me when you have finished," and she walks away homeward.

"We may perhaps go on till dinner time," replies Euphemia demurely; but the instant that her mother is out of sight she tosses away the book, and springing out of the hammock, slips away into the shrubberies, followed by the other two. She keeps ahead of them, and at the path's first elbow disappears.

The maneuver is so patent that for a moment it makes both those who benefit by it feel awkward. But in Clarence's case it is only for a moment. This is one of his life's big moments, and he must wring his destiny out of it. But he has never in his life before asked a woman to marry him, and he has not the remotest idea how to begin.

"Was it anywhere near here that you found your wren's nest?"

"No, oh, no! that was in a fir tree, and these are all hardwood ones. What a pity"—looking up—"that there is such a plague of caterpillars on the oaks this year!"

"Yes, isn't it?"

"But it has one advantage. It brings a great many more nightingales."

"Do they eat caterpillars?"

"Yes."

It was hardly worth while to have fled for privacy into the heart of a wood in order to exchange remarks of the above kind. This thought puts a kind of rage into his next sentence.

"Are we to spend our last walk in talking of caterpillars?"

There is no rage in her answer :

"I think one has dropped on my neck at the back. Would you mind taking it off?"

She stoops her large-hatted little head as she speaks, and presents to him her nape, on which, sure enough, a many legged wanderer is expatiating. It is with very mixed feelings that the lover picks off the little green wriggler. He feels the confidingness of the request in one whom her unhappy experience of men has made so stand-off, and not all his reverence can quell a strong thrill at this first, perhaps last, contact with the warm satin of her skin ; but yet, that at such a moment she should be able to talk of a caterpillar !

"I thought you would have cared,—a little!"

Her answer is almost inaudible :

"I never care a *little* about anything."

He is still pondering the enigma of this sentence, when a turn in the path brings them into close view of its end, and a moment later they are looking down at the sunk fence that bars their further progress. It is overhung by a giant elm, iron-clamped, to hinder the two halves, like separate trees, of its prodigious bulk from leaning further and further apart, surprising, by its majesty, those who come suddenly into sight of it. Under its boughs they must needs halt. This pause gives him at least the advantage of a little command of her face, standing opposite, instead of beside her.

"You never care a little about anything?" he repeats. "Does that mean that you ever care a great deal?"

"I have never had anything much to care about," she answers; and though she does not intend it, the words ring forlornly.

"But if you *had* anything to care about, would you care about it *much?*"

The question sounds in his own ears ridiculously like, "If you had a brother, would he like cheese?" but her sense of the absurd is not very quick, and she only answers, almost under her breath:

"Perhaps."

Interpreting her one word in the sense he would have it, he can no longer govern himself, but stretches out his arms to enfold her "small but ravishing substance." But she gives a start and eludes him, while her eyes, downcast till now, throw a deeply reproachful look at him.

In the almost mechanical gesture of self-defense he reads afresh the melancholy story of her past experience of men. It is an archaic solecism nowadays to ask kneeling for the hand of any lady; but he can think of no better way to show the extremity of his reverence for her than by kneeling to her on the mossed grass. In this attitude, and taking her hand, he says with the deepest respect:

"Will you be my dear and honored wife?"

It is a mode of offering himself that savors more of the eighteenth than the nineteenth century, but she does not know much about the eighteenth century, and her lip quivers. Looking up into the stirred depths of her velvet eyes, and realizing more than ever the small whiteness of her pensive yet plucky little face, and of what a gallant heart it is the index, he must needs change his key. A line of the quaint Elizabethan lyric which had put Lady Bramshill to flight comes to his aid. He has laid his other hand over her already pinioned one, and the passion which a divine pity and longing to protect her had for the moment stirred and awed comes swelling back into his voice in a sort of laugh:

"'Hast thou any mind of me?'"

An agitated smile breaks doubtful at first, then like morning's red promise, over her face, and in a tiny voice comes the answering verse:

"'I have even great mind of thee!' You see, I do know *one* line of poetry!" with a little sob; and so, he still kneeling to receive her, she stoops forward with "rosy pudency" into his blessed arms.

But it is not long before she withdraws herself from his embrace, the inveterate habit of reserve reasserting itself. She only leaves him her hand as a pledge of not slipping from him altogether, and when she speaks her voice is troubled:

"Do you realize that I have been very badly brought up?"

"Fully."

"Are you quite sure that you understand *how* badly? Had I not better tell you now?"

"Not now! Not now!"

"I think it would be more honest to tell you!"

"Then be dishonest."

"Will it—will it—hurt her very much?"

"Hurt whom?"

For the moment, lapt in Elysium, he has actually forgotten.

"Your mother."

The wings with which he has been soaring to heaven drop off. He cannot tell her the truth, and he cannot lie to her; but she reads the answer in his face. She heaves a sigh.

"Must one always buy one's happiness with some-one else's pain?"

He can think of no better answer than to unclasp the one hand she has left him and lift its palm—a little hardened by much wielding of golf clubs—to his lips. She allows the action, but with a slight flush, then speaks again:

"And she has not been used to being unhappy, has she?"

"No, not for many years. Thank God, no!"

A little pause.

"It must be so much worse to be unhappy when you are not used to it," she says softly.

"Does that mean that you are used to it?"

"I have always been rather unhappy," she answers matter-of-factly.

A wave of immense tenderness toward both his beloveds pours from his heart over his lips.

"You shall never, either of you, have a moment's unhappiness again!" he cries rationally.

CHAPTER XII.

THAT there are difficulties in the way of keeping that half of his promise which refers to his mother, Clarence feels pretty clearly as he nears his home late that night—late, for the Bramshills, like most Indians, are a sitting-up family, and he has to be almost turned out even then. Yet, after they leave the wood, he enjoys very little of his love's company, thanks less to his fear of Lady Bramshill's raillery than to Honor's earnest desire that the Bramshill family should not learn the state of the case until she has obtained her father's consent.

To disguise his balked longings, he throws himself into the semblance of a furious devotion to Euphemia, which, with inward laughter, she goes quite halfway to meet.

He has made up his mind to let his mother have the night's reprieve, when the sight of a light under her bedroom door as he passes it upsets his resolution. He knocks, and her voice, perfectly wakeful, bids him come in. A slight noise of rustling tells him as he does so that she has risen from her knees. "Is she *always* praying?" is his thought, made up in equal parts of the old awed tenderness at her saintliness, and the new irritated wonder for what boon she can be so ceaselessly besieging her God.

She knows that it annoys him to find her kneeling,

and makes a little feint, which gives him a prick of conscience, of having been sitting all along in her armchair. But a tell-tale manual of devotion left open on the back of her *prie-dieu* betrays her.

His eye rests, disturbed, yet tender, upon the heading of one of the prayers: " For a Departed Friend."

"You pray for—for my father still?"

If she answers at all, it is by a slight assenting motion of the head ; but her words have no relation to the subject.

"How quietly you came in! I never heard the hall door. Were you afraid of waking your old mother? I need not ask "—taking his face with jealous fondness into her two hands as he stoops to kiss her—" whether you have enjoyed yourself."

"Do I radiate light?" he asks excitedly. "I am sure I *ought!* But I did not know "—with a laugh—"that it was written all over me *outside!*"

He hopes she will ask what "it" is; but no. That she guesses is evident by the slow subsiding of her framing hands from his face down into her lap. But it is not a little thing that can rebut him to-night. Perhaps he may take her by storm.

He falls on his knees beside her, and enwraps her in his arms.

"My mother! All my life you have been very glad when I have been even a little glad; now that I am *very* glad, will not you be even a little glad?"

Her self-control gives way.

"*Glad!* GLAD!" she repeats, pressing her face with a moan against his shoulder. Then, feeling his arms slackening, she makes a great effort to pull herself together. " I must know first what I have to be glad about, must not I ? "

The sound of that wail in her voice has chilled away the hot words of boiling happiness from his lips.

" Did you give my message to Miss Lisle ? Is she coming to see me ? I dare say we shall find plenty to talk about after all. You must explain to her that I am that most foolish of anomalies, a shy old woman! "

He recognizes the heroic effort that this *amende* has cost her, but his gratitude is lost in pain at the perceptible intensity of her inward revolt.

He frees her from that hold which he had hoped might have caressed her into at least acquiescence, and sits down on a chair at a politer and less tender distance.

" I am afraid the visit cannot be paid *this* time. Miss Lisle has been sent for home by her father, and has to leave The Beeches early to-morrow morning." Though he is not looking at her, intuition and the sound of a slight start telling him of the flash of joy and hope that this piece of news has sent racing through her being, he hurries on: " But, as you often say, '*Ce qui est différé, n'est point perdu*'; and before long I—I—hope to bring her to you *for good!* "

In his excitement he has drawn his chair nearer to her, leaning forward the while, so as to diminish still further the distance between them, and the two faces, so unlike, and yet on both which extreme emotion is drawing out the latent likeness, peer into each other.

He is not sure, so low is it spoken, but he thinks that she repeats his two last words, "*for good*," with an accent of exquisite irony.

"She has promised to marry me."

Not even a repetition of his words this time. Once again his arms are round her. He cannot believe that the talisman of his touch—which, when he was little, would have wiled the heart out of her body, and has seemed only to gain in power as the reserve of manhood has made his endearments rarer—can have utterly lost its effect.

"Mother, you do not want me to go through life *wifeless*, do you?—you, that have yourself known the blessedness of a happy marriage!"

He feels her writhe in his embrace. Is it for this that she has practiced upon him the pious fraud of concealing the ugly wretchedness of her own experience of the nuptial tie?

But he mistakes the cause of her involuntary gesture, and, once again loosing her, rises and stands beside her.

"You are not treating me well," he says, in a voice of profound, though partially controlled, indignation. "With what difference could you have received my news if I had brought you as daughter an *outcast*—a—a—Poppy de Vere?"

"You misunderstand me," she says faintly, stretching out her hand to draw him back. "You must not run away with an idea."

"Do you think that I want to?" he asks, half

mollified. "But I felt you distinctly shudder at the mention of my marriage with her. What could you have done more had it——"

"You are mistaken," she interrupts. "I was not thinking of the present, but of—of—the *past!*"

He is back in a moment at her knees.

"The *past!* Oh, poor mother! But I hoped that that old wound had long ago healed."

"So it has—so it has. *You*"—embracing him feverishly with her slender arms—"have healed *all* my wounds long, *long* ago. But you know that old wounds have a trick of breaking out afresh after many years."

"Yes, yes, of course"—remorsefully.

"You must not be in a hurry with me"—tremulously. "You know that I cannot go quite as fast as you. I am old and slow."

"Her first thought was for you—her first question whether you would be hurt."

"Was it?"

"She said——"

The mother breaks in, as if her ears could not yet endure the sound of the enamored quotation:

"Yes, yes; I am sure she said everything that was nice."

"She knows that you dislike her."

"Does she?"

"And is anxious—touchingly anxious—to propitiate you."

"Is she?"

"She consulted me as to how best to do it."

"Did she? And what did you advise?"

"I gave her the same advice as you have just given me—not to hurry you. I told her that you are slow to like, but that when you do love it is for time and eternity. Was I right?"

There is the old reverent enthusiasm back in his voice, but its return gives her no joy.

"I do not quite know," she answers, turning about her head miserably. "One does not quite know about one's self, does one?"

"As I have always told you, you are so strangely alike in essentials,"—she gives a slight start of distaste, but it is so slight that she trusts he is not aware of it,—"under your surface unlikenesses, that I do not think it is humanly possible that you can fail to grow dear to one another."

"Isn't it?"

"In six months"—warming with his theme—"you will be as fond of her as she is already prepared to be of you."

"I dare say"—in an almost extinct voice.

"You will have two people to love you instead of one."

This foolish little multiplication sum has no sooner passed his lips than he feels its futility. She bursts into uncontrollable tears, which drop scalding upon his neck.

"I have always been quite, *quite* satisfied with my *one*."

The poor soul had meant to have behaved so well, and she has not behaved very well after all!

Her recognition of his news is not such as to incline him to seek with her consolation for his love's departure when the early train has steamed away with her on the following morning, and without much pressing he goes back with the Bramshills, who have mustered in force to see her off, and so innocently marred the privacy of his adieu, to breakfast at The Beeches.

Though forbidden to tell them of his bliss, yet the long loudness of their laments over their departed guest makes him feel as perfectly in tune with them as he is out of tune with his home surroundings, and in Euphemia's eye, at least, he reads perfect knowledge.

"I am *lost* without her," she says, in a tone of such affectionate exaggeration as sends a grateful beam from his eye to hers; and Lady Bramshill adds with a sigh:

"Yes, she is a dear little oddity, and has managed to creep into all our hearts."

It gives the young man rather a shock to hear his divinity alluded to as a "dear little oddity," and Euphemia evidently reads his thought, for she says, with a smile in the tail of her fine eye:

"You must come to dinner to-night to cheer us up. We shall be as flat as pancakes without our 'oddity' if you do not."

Her look at him is so full of comprehension and goodwill that it is a very faint demurrer which he puts in:

"I should like it, of all things, more than I can say. The only objection is, that I do not quite like to leave my mother two nights running."

Though the objection is evidently only offered to be overruled, Lady Bramshill takes it up with more haste than hospitality.

"You are quite right. We must not be selfish, and lead you into neglecting your mother; and as you very properly say, she would be sadly lonely without you."

"It is a condition of mind which *we* cannot understand, mother," rejoins Euphemia sub-impertinently; "but Mrs. Clarence likes to be alone. She told me so herself, in the hope, I think,"—with a teasing smile,—"that I should pass on the information to you. No, no,"—to the young man,—"you may put your filial piety into your pocket, and come."

His own inclination is so much on her side that he does not notice that the daughter's invitation is unindorsed by the lady of the house, and he accepts.

A week passes, of which most of the hours that he can spare from his work are spent at that spot where, though he can no longer hope to find his love in bodily presence, he may yet, with the fine eye and ear of fancy, trace her small footsteps and catch the echo of her strange little voice. Sometimes Euphemia stalks in silent sympathy by his side; sometimes he steals off alone to the forked elm at the thicket end, and lives over again, in hot, tranced memory, his life's prime half-hour.

A week has passed, and she has not yet taken the embargo off his tongue. He has received from her, in answer to his outpourings, three stiff little notes, chiefly occupied by apologies for her penmanship and spelling, and by explanations that she has not yet found a fitting moment for calling her father's attention—evidently always of the slackest—to her affairs.

All three billets are stiff; but the last is illumined by a rather indistinct postscript: "Do not make me get *too* fond of you." He kisses the trembling line illegible.

As ill-luck will have it, all three notes have been given him in the presence of his mother, and he has sheepishly conveyed them unread to his pocket. She has looked on, or rather carefully away, in silence in the case of the two first, but at the third she speaks in an unsure voice:

"Will not you read your letter?"

One look at her tells him what the request has cost her to make.

"Oh, thanks! I will, then, if you will let me."

He would like to take it at least to the window, where he might gloat and beam over it unnoticed; but she looks so ostentatiously in another direction that he does not like to wound her by changing his position. Yet as he reads, he knows that she has not been able to resist one snatched glance at him, and that it has reached him just as the flash of shy passion in the postscript had sent an unveilable glow over his features. He makes for the door.

"I may be detained," he says, stopping a second on his way out; "do not wait dinner for me."

Her movements are usually so slow in their noiseless grace that he is not prepared to find her at the door before him; but there she stands, with her back to it, one white hand pressed against the panel behind her.

"You shall not go!" she says, in a key of quivering command. "I will not let you! You shall not go to pour out your heart to those—those upstart strangers, while you keep it shut to me!"

There is such an anguish of jealousy and hurt-to-death love in her voice that once again, as so often of late, alternating with resentment, there rushes a billow of reverent pity over his heart.

"You are mistaken," he answers. "I have told them nothing. You are my only confidante, as you have been all my life; and, besides, she has forbidden me to tell anyone until she has obtained her father's consent."

"Is there any likelihood of his refusing it?"

If he recognizes an involuntary hope in the breathlessness of her voice, he hastens to quench it.

"Not the slightest. He will be thankful to be rid of her."

He dislikes the phrase as soon as uttered, since there is an apparent belittling of his love's value in it.

"I should be only too glad if you would tell me a little about her. You—you used to like to have me for a listener."

The humble appeal of her tone, showing the fullness of her surrender, touches him to the quick.

"The wide world could not give me anything I should like better."

He passes his arm around her as he speaks, and draws her head to his shoulder. It lies there peaceably for only a moment. She lifts it restlessly.

"Tell me *now, here, now!* Do not go away!"

"I am afraid that I must," he answers soothingly, and still caressing her. "Lady Bramshill has something that she wishes to say to me,—I cannot conceive *what,*—and has appointed this hour; but I will not stay a moment longer than I can help, and then—then——"

. . . . .

It is with an inexpressibly light heart that the young man canters across the pastures of the now so familiar short-cut to The Beeches. Fortune is showering her goods on him with both hands. If she will only add to her liberality that of making Lady Bramshill short-winded! A transient wonder crosses his mind—it has done so several times before—as to what communication she can have to make to him that needs the pomp of an appointment. But his heart is too full of joy to have much leisure to pause over it.

He leaves his horse at the stables, and, reaching the house, is shown at once upstairs into Lady Bramshill's private room, into which he has never before penetrated. She is apparently waiting for him, sitting on a sofa, and with no visible occupation. There is a constraint, which surprises him, in her manner of greeting and complimenting him on his punctuality.

"Am I so punctual? I was afraid that I was a little late."

"No, no! Quite punctual."

"I think I understood that you wished to speak——"

She cuts off the tail of his sentence.

"How is your mother?"

"She is pretty well, thanks. She feels the heat a good deal—at least, she looks pale."

"Looks pale, does she? Has she been worried about anything lately? Has she had anything to worry her?"

He hesitates.

"She has had nothing that she *need* worry about."

While he is speaking his companion has got up to draw aside and look behind a hanging of Indian grass-cloth which screens a recess of the room.

"These *portières* are such treacherous things, one has no security that someone is not listening to us."

The evident agitation of her manner is beginning to make him feel uncomfortable, though he would be puzzled to say why.

"Would it matter"—smiling—"if they were seven deep at the keyhole, like the servants at Sir Pitt Crawley's proposal?"

She comes back.

"There is no one there, but perhaps it would be safer if we did not speak very loud."

His vague disquietude grows more acute.

"What can you have to say to me that requires such secrecy?" he asks, in a voice of suppressed ridicule, and only half-suppressed irritation.

Again she rises and walks to a window, which she shuts.

"Voices carry so far through an open window."

"I must beg you"—civilly, yet imperatively, too—"not to delay any longer telling me what it is that needs so much mystery as a preamble."

"I will, I will!" her flurry palpably increasing. "Of course, I have no right to keep you in suspense; but it is such a very difficult thing to say—to put into words—liking you as I do, and your mother before you. You believe how much we have all liked you?"

"*Have* liked!" repeats he, struck by her employment of the past tense. "Are you going to tell me that I have done anything to forfeit your liking?"

"No, oh, no! At least, not intentionally, I am sure."

"Unintentionally, then?"

"I know that your mother's son must be, and is, the soul of honor."

"*Honor!*" repeats he, growing deeply red. "Do you mean to imply that there is any question of my having behaved dishonorably?"

"No, no! You must not run away with an idea. I am sure that nothing was further from your thoughts; but you have just been drifting."

A light—a disagreeable one—breaks upon him. This officious fat woman is going to take him to task about his conduct toward his darling. Well, perhaps, having no more knowledge than she has upon the subject, she is only doing her duty. She may, with some show of reason, suppose that he is trifling with her affections. He smiles involuntarily at the grotesqueness of this idea. It is an innocent smile enough, but its effect is unfortunate.

"It may be a laughing matter to you," says his companion, and he sees that indignation has superseded the distress hitherto reigning on her good-natured face—"it may be a laughing matter to you, but I assure you it is none to me."

He hesitates, undecided how to clear himself from

the imputation brought against him without disobeying his dear lady's commands, and with an outgoing of real friendliness toward the fussy, hot woman, who, at the expense of much unpleasantness to herself, is so bravely mothering his little motherless treasure.

His hesitation gives her time and, apparently, inclination, for she goes on more fluently than hitherto to take up her parable again :

"You may ask why I have not spoken to *her*, but if you knew the ins and outs of things, you would allow that it is not so easy. I have tried to approach the subject once or twice, and she has treated me with derision—absolute derision ! "

"*Derision !*" repeats he, in indignant defense of the absent. "How unlike her! She is always so scrupulously courteous ! "

His partisanship seems to heighten her ire.

"Perhaps *you* may find her so ; though in the beginning I have seen her not very civil to you."

"I certainly never perceived it "—wounded.

"I do not want to say anything against her ; she is a very good girl in the main, but headstrong is not the word for her ! If once she takes the bit between her teeth, it is all over. Well, we have no one to thank but ourselves. We have spoiled her desperately. I suppose it is often the case with Indian children. We had to be separated from her for so long that when we did see her we felt we could not make enough of her."

She stops, and he sees tears in her eyes ; but any compassion he might feel for her is drowned in the flood of light as to her meaning that pours over him. It is, then, her own daughter Euphemia in whose defense against him she has been ruffling her feathers and sharpening her beak.

Ludicrous as the misconception appears to him, he feels at once that it is a perfectly natural one, and a relief that his own sacred secret is still intact, mingled with a doubt as to how to keep it so while clearing himself from the accusation brought against him, gives her time to go on:

"When we have discussed the subject of her marriage, she has always given us plainly to understand that she means to consult her own wishes, not ours, in the matter; and, within certain limits, we perfectly acquiesce."

"And you do not consider that I come within these limits?" again reddening, and more intensely than before.

She looks at him with what he sees to be a perfectly unput-on astonishment.

"I do not know why you should force me to say these painful things to you; but I must really refer you to your own common sense for an answer."

A flash of angry amusement darts across him at the absurdity of the mistake which has made him so unpleasantly acquainted with Lady Bramshill's opinion of her social superiority to him—for what other meaning can attach to her sentence? But the good manners so early instilled into him make him try to keep both out of his voice.

"You are laboring under an entire misconception. The idea of winning Miss Bramshill's affections has never once crossed my mind, nor, I am very sure, hers either; so I think you will see the needlessness of any further pointing out to me what presumption it would have been in me if I had entertained such a thought."

She is looking at him again with the same unaffected astonishment, only acuter than before.

"*Presumption!* What does the man mean? You talk as if you did not know what I was alluding to."

"I think you made your meaning sufficiently clear—that you did not think me worthy of the honor of being connected with you."

The red, of which he has not, even so far, had a monopoly, spreads from her good-natured and now deeply distressed face to her neck.

"Great Heavens! Talk of mistakes! You are making one with a vengeance now! *Presumption!* Why, do you think that there is any young man whom I should have been so ready to take to my heart as you? so steady as you are; your relations to your mother so beautiful; getting on so well in your profession; the son of my dear old friend—if——"

"If what?"

The hopeless mystification in which he has been floundering is growing tinged by a vague alarm.

"If it were not for the one dreadful, *dreadful* drawback."

"What drawback are you alluding to?"

She goes close up to him, and lowers her voice:

"You do not know? No, I see you do not. Is it possible, and have *I* to tell you?"

"If you please."

He knows that a blow is coming, and has the manly impulse to string himself up to bear it pluckily.

She is quite near him, and he can see pulses growing in her throat, and her lips moving in the effort to comply ; but apparently she cannot manage it.

"It is impossible!" is all that she can bring out at last. "You must get someone else to tell you—your mother."

"*You* must tell me."

She had begun to sidle doorward ; but his tone, for he uses no other method of compulsion, arrests her. She sinks her voice and braces herself.

"I took it for granted—very stupidly, I own, for people whom they may concern are always the last to hear things—that you must be aware of the—the——"

"The what?"

"The terrible curse—disease—that is hereditary in your family."

"What curse? What disease?"

"The disease of—insanity."

A beam of relieved incredulity darts across him. Here must be a second error, absurder than the first. Were there this deadly malady inherent in his blood, would his mother have allowed him to blunder on in the dark all his life, ignorant of and unprovided with the armor of foreknowledge against so hideous a foe? Impossible!

"Are you sure that you are not mistaken—that you are not confounding us with some other family?"

Probably the unbelief of his tone, try as he may to veil it with politeness, gives her the impetus necessary to complete her task.

"I wish to God that I were! But, unfortunately,

since I lived from infancy in the immediate neighborhood of your family, that is not possible. Your father died in a lunatic asylum, as did his two brothers and his sister, as did his father and grandfather before him." She pauses to take breath, but no fresh expression of incredulity reaches her ears. "It is, unhappily, one of the best authenticated cases of hereditary homicidal mania on record, and has been quoted as such repeatedly in medical journals." She has done her work effectually this time. He stands before her dumb and blanched—*so* dumb, *so* blanched, that her tongue falters over her next words: "I—I—thought—I took it for granted that you knew."

She may continue or leave her halting apology. He neither knows nor cares whether she adds another stone or two to the cairn she has built upon his heart. But the instinct of civility still survives.

"At least, I know now," he says, with a smile, which she is not fond of remembering afterward. "I am obliged to you for having enlightened me, and I quite agree with you that I should not be a desirable son-in-law."

CHAPTER XIII.

WHEN he goes to his grave Clarence will be scarcely less conscious of the transit than he is of how he gets home. The ride across the fields is a blank, except that at one spot, where he skirts the edge of a hayfield, the smell of the new-cut grass recalls to him a thought of peculiar sweetness that had crossed his mind as he passed it on his way to The Beeches.

When the air has carried away the balmy waft, he relapses into blank, with no feeling beyond that of an impulse to get home with the least possible delay; though if anyone had asked him the reason of his hurry, he is probably stunned enough to have been puzzled to give one. Happily, he meets, and is consequently questioned by, no one.

His mother is not at church. The thought that she might be so had struck him with a vague rage of fear. Had she been so, he must have dragged her even from the altar foot to answer him. Neither is she in her oratory. She is in the drawing room, quietly working, with a heap of colored silks making a rainbow beside her, while she listens with a slight, absent smile to Abigail's communications from the window.

"Someone has come to stay with the Mitchells. She has given the parlor maid the fare to pay the cabman. He will not take it; it is not enough. She evidently thinks that it is a shilling fare. Ah! she has given him another sixpence. He is driving off."

Mrs. Clarence's face turns toward her son as he enters, like a sunflower to the sun—ludicrous comparison for anything so palely small! For the first time for weeks, it wears no apprehension of seeing coldness or aversion on his. But the moment that her eye encounters his it loses its light. He stands beside her, with his back to the girl at the window, for the first moment so speechless that she asks him in a frightened whisper:

"What is it?"

Then he finds enough voice to answer:

"I must speak to you alone—now—not here."

She rises without a word, and follows him out of the room, the unconscious Abigail's voice sounding in their singing ears. He leads, and she follows, down to the smoking room, whose French window stands open to the little back garden. Through it a mat of white pinks is sending the sun-warmed spice of its fragrance. Opposite the window they both come to a standstill, and look, pale and hard, at each other—she with a dull, terrified sense of some enormous overhanging woe, he as if without words he would force an answer to his unspoken, almost unspeakable, question. He fails. She remains mute in her trembling before him, and he puts his dread into speech.

"Is it true?"

"Is what true?"

"Do you mean to say that you do not know to what I am alluding?"

"No, I do not."

Her looks are as of one on the edge of a swoon, and her denial is hardly audible. Yet he draws a tiny drop of comfort from it. She is a rigorously truthful woman, and it *is* a denial.

"That—my father—died—in a mad-house?"

His key is no higher than hers. She gives a sort of stagger; but so she would were she hearing for the first time a terrific calumny.

"Who—told—you—so?"

The form of the rejoinder puts his sick hopes to death.

"Lady Bramshill."

She has leaned for a moment as if to prop herself against the window shutter, but at his answer she stands upright again, and a light of blazing indignation such as he has never before seen in them flares out from her great tragic eyes.

"*Lady Bramshill! His own son! How dared she!*"

"She was perfectly right from her point of view. She imagined that I wanted to marry her daughter. But what does all that matter?" pushing his own explanation aside. "Is it true?"

Her little wrists are manacled almost brutally by his hands. He has forgotten compassion, forgotten reverence, forgotten love. He remembers only that hideous fear. She is to him for the moment only the mouthpiece of destiny, the machine by which he is to be made or unmade.

To her the idea has not the dreadful novelty that it has to him. Her mind is even capable of the flashed thought of how true an intuition had been her apparently incommensurate dread and dislike of the renewed acquaintance of her youth. Then, recognizing that what she has darkly feared for him for five-and-twenty years has now irrecoverably befallen him, her lips form a lifeless but unmistakable "Yes."

"That he died in a mad-house?"

"Yes."

"That his father before him did the same?"

"Yes."

"That it is a case of hereditary lunacy?"

"Yes."

"And that it is—*homicidal?*"

"Yes."

Her five yeses are at first only five words knocking at the door of his brain, but after a moment or two they are let in. He gives a sort of lurch, and her hands tumble out of his suddenly loosed grasp. She thinks he is about to fall, and, snatching at his arm, leads him—since a momentary blindness seems to have come over him—to a chair. Then she falls on her knees beside him, and with her handkerchief wipes the cold sweat that stands out on his brow. Our instincts survive our reason, as we all know, and a vague surface sense of unfitness in the humility of her attitude plays over the chaos of his mind.

"Thank you, mother, thank you! But, please, do not trouble; I—I am all—right."

So they remain a while, he sitting upright, staring straight in front of him; she kneeling humbly, with all her riven heart in her great eyes, beside him. At length he speaks:

"Did you know it when you married him?"

"Oh, no, no!"

"Did your guardian know it?"

"He must have done."

"You were only seventeen?"

"Yes."

Another silence. The blind look has gone out of his eyes, and his mind is shaking off its paralysis. He is evidently piecing together fragments of the past, clearing up long ago intelligibilities, joining them on to the present.

"That was why you never would go out into the world?"

"Ye-es."

Another pause—more piecing.

"That was why you were always in such terror at the idea of my marriage?"

Her lips move; but, no doubt to save him pain, or perhaps because her powers of endurance are giving way, the assent which they frame is not even so decided a one as its hesitating predecessor.

"And I"—with an accent of bitterest self-reproach—"could attribute it to a paltry jealousy!"

Again her lips stir, but produce nothing. For the moment his mind, happily for him, has lost sight of his own abysmal fall, and is running in the track of his misdoings.

"I used the argument of your own happy married life to reconcile you to mine!"

To defend him against his self-accusations, she recovers voice:

"You did not know—how could you?"

A new interval of silence.

"How soon did you find it out?"

"About six months after I married."

"*It*,"—his voice has sunk to a whisper—"it came on in paroxysms?"

"Yes."

"With intervals of perfect sanity between?"

"Yes."

"When it—when it came on first, did he—did he ill-use you?"

She hesitates.

"He was not accountable."

"He was in—confinement for the greater part of your married life?"

"No, only on and off for the last half year."

"You kept him at home up to then?"

"Yes."

"At the peril of your life?"

"I was not much afraid."

Again, even at this moment, but now in tantalizing misery, the idea of the intrinsic likeness between his mother and his love darts across him.

"Was there any warning of the attacks coming on?"

"I grew to know the signs."

"And you carried your life daily and nightly for four and a half years at a madman's mercy?"

"Yes."

"With no one to share your burden?"

"Your nurse, Nasmyth, knew."

"You did it because you loved him."

Hitherto she has answered like a machine, with

lifeless precision; but her son's last sentence is a statement, not a question, so it naturally goes unanswered.

He lifts her off her knees, as if there were sacrilege in her adoption of such an attitude toward himself.

"Mother! mother! I always knew that you were one of God's saints; but I did not know till now that you were one of his martyrs, too!"

And then the two poor smitten creatures cling together a while, and mix the bitter water of their tears. But, though the tidings are old to her, and new to him, hers are beyond measure the bitterest.

It is not till he has had the enormity of a whole perfectly sleepless night in which to measure it that he realizes the size of his calamity,—that he recognizes it in all its bearings,—knows that it is commensurate with his whole future life.

His mother does not appear at breakfast, and he has to face Abigail's babble alone. He even eats eggs and bacon without choking, and echoes her puerile suppositions as to her neighbors' affairs, though across his mind at the same moment is darting the grotesquely horrible wonder whether it is safe for her to breakfast *tête-à-tête* with him.

It is not till noon that Mrs. Clarence opens the door of the smoking room, and gives him the shock of seeing what his discovery of her secret has cost her. In her eyes he reads that her own consternation at the change in his appearance is not less. He takes her in his arms with the tenderest compassion.

"You poor soul! you have not slept?"

Her eyelids quiver.

"'Macbeth hath murdered sleep!'" she answers, with a little stony smile.

"And yet to you it is no new thing; and as to *me*,"—with a look of braced nerves,—"thank God for having let me learn it *in time!*"

"*In time?*"

"It is an ill-wind"—with an exceeding bitter little laugh—"that blows nobody any good. You are secure now that no one will ever rob you of your precious son!" Then, as she looks at him with only a dawning of comprehension: "I must go and tell her to-day. It is not a thing that one could very well *write*, and I"—a slight uncertainty in the hitherto well sustained tone—"I should like to see her once again."

His mother has been lying, with a half-extinguished look, in a long chair; but at his words she raises herself.

"You are going to tell her?"

"Yes."

"And you think,"—is her accent one of incredulity, or hope, or only mere wretchedness?—"and you think —you believe—that she will give you up?"

"I am as certain as that I stand here,"—the woe of his face made almost bright by a quick light of confident love,—"that she will not."

"Then——"

"I shall not give her the chance."

The sudden drop of his tone, the return—tenfold intensified by its second of illumination—of the outer darkness in his face, rouse her.

"Do nothing in a hurry!" she cries, with a hoarse tremble in her voice. "Wait a little. If her father is so anxious to be rid of her,—if her home is so unhappy——"

But the sternness of his look as he almost pushes her from him makes her falter away into silence.

"You are forgetting what a marriage-gift I bring my wife!"

"There must be an end to it some time or other," she says, in a breathless whisper; "the curse must wear out in time. Why not *now?* Why not with *you; you,* who have always been so faultlessly healthy and sound in mind and body; *you,* who have never had ache or pain since the day of your birth"—the pride of a lifetime piercing even now through the misery of her tone; "*you,* whom people used to stop in the street when you were a little child to admire your strength and your beauty; *you,* who, from one side at least, inherit no smallest taint?" Her speech has grown rapider and rapider, and by this time she has tightly enlaced him with her arms. "Do nothing yet! I adjure you, *wait, wait!*"

She stops exhausted, but still convulsively pressing him in her arms, as if to force consent out of him by the strenuousness of that embrace.

Even at this moment he is capable of a wonder-struck thought that the frenzy of her supplication is directed toward preventing his giving up that relation, her distaste for which had gone nigh to making the only breach in their lives between them.

The recognition of the utter unselfishness of her pleading adds one more pang of bitter tenderness to the sum of his affection for her. He puts his hand very softly, though resolutely, over her mouth.

"Mother," he says, "you would not make it harder for me, would you? You know as well as I do that, having learned what I have learned, it would be a crime in me to marry *any* woman."

Something in his tone tells her that her implorings are vain. Her arms drop away from him. She is so little used to be demonstrative. It is the measure of her woe that it has betrayed her into a manifestation so contrary to her nature.

Heavily, heavily once again silence wraps them.

"It will be better to get it over," he says at last, the old habit of deference to her wishes making his tone even now apologetic for this contravention of them. "I have looked out my train. I shall go to-night, and see her to-morrow morning."

"Where does she live?"

"In Limeshire."

"I ought to have known," she says, in a faint voice of self-reproach; "I ought to have asked more about her."

"It does not matter now," he answers calmly, and, so swallowed up are all lesser emotions in the ocean of his despair, without the least tinge of resentment.

. . . . .

His train reaches the North Country station for which he is bound at too early an hour for him to present himself at once. He walks to a railway inn, washes, dresses, and forces himself to eat; then, hiring a dog-cart, drives the three miles that he is told intervene between him and the object of his quest.

At the gate of an apparently untenanted lodge he stops, and, dismissing his vehicle, enters a park whose grass-grown drive and neglected timber evidence the moneylessness or indifference of its owner.

He has traversed more than a mile before he comes in sight of a large, bald Georgian house, which, as he approaches it, he sees to be, in the ugly fashion of that day, unbrightened by any surrounding garden. He mounts a *perron* and rings a bell, but he has plenty of time to admire the blistered paint of the portal before any answer comes to his summons. When it does, the sound of withdrawing bolts, and the sight of an obvious charwoman, at once tell him that the brief visit of the Comus of the house with his satyrs is a thing of the past, and gives him time for a flash of—is it dread or hope?—that the daughter of the house may be absent too.

But the woman takes his card, and, marking her consciousness of his not being a *dun* by requesting him to walk in, she leaves him standing in a great square hall, the cold tessellation of whose pavement is relieved by no carpet or rug, and surrounded by sheeted forms of furniture. Half-open doors giving into large adjoining apartments reveal further seas of holland. Is it possible that amid this state of utter dismantlement anyone can be living?

He is left to ponder this question for some time after the charwoman's feet have echoed off into the void; but it plays only on the surface of his mind, which has no room for aught within it but the leaden weight of the errand on which he has come. Yet, unconsciously, the manifest signs of decay around him—even the dirt of the cornice, to which he idly lifts his wandering look—add to the sum of his misery, since it was from all this, and what it figures, that he was to have rescued her.

He must have been left to his speculations for a quarter of an hour before the sound of a foot—a different one from that of his first introducer—falls on his ear. It is light, and it comes along with even swiftness; then it runs down naked marble stairs; then it walks, springy and glad, across the black and white diamonds of the floor; then it stops at his side.

He dares hardly lift his look to the sober little face—sober, as he knows, only from its effort to mask the expression of a too bubbling joy.

"They could not find me at first," says a voice, sober too, from the same cause as the face. "I was setting off to the kennels to see the young entry. I am glad that they overtook me."

He cannot answer or explain. It is worse than he had expected. The sight of that small embodiment of modest, grave felicity, with the knowledge of what is in store for her, holds him dumb.

A slight look of surprise just passes over her bright face, but it is gone in a second.

"Do not stay here. Come to the schoolroom."

She turns to lead the way, looking, amid the misshapen, shrouded forms coldly white around her, like "Love among the Ruins." As she walks along ahead of him, she says, in a voice that he feels to be crestfallen:

"It does not look very comfortable; but there are not many servants."

It is evident that she is attributing his silence to dismay at her surroundings. Even when he becomes conscious of this, he cannot find words to remove the impression.

They go echoing along miles of cold corridors and acres of tenantless, wrapped rooms, till a loudly resounding naked stair leads them to a door which gives entrance into what is evidently an older part of the house. The passages are still carpetless, but their narrower size makes them several degrees less loftily dreary than those already traversed.

His guide at length pauses at a room door, and passes in before him, and then turns, with a rather diffident smile, to welcome him to her domain.

"If I had known you were coming, I would have tried to make things look a little more cheerful."

She is still crestfallen, under the influence of that misapprehension, and eyes with a certain deprecation her paintless bower, with its threadbare carpet and decrepit chairs. He must speak.

"I did not know it myself."

"Whether you were expected or not, you are very, *very* welcome!" she says, with a sweet little formality. "Will not you sit down?"

He knows that in the depth of her maidenly heart she must be marveling at his stockfish immobility—marveling why she is not in his arms! He has been in a measure stupefied hitherto, but now a stream of anguish runs like melted lead over his heart at the thought that what he has come to tell her is that she will never, *never* lie in them again!

Oh, why not once, *once* again? He cannot communicate his curse to her in one last solemn kiss; *last*—not in the petulant sense used by hasty lovers parting for a day, a week, a month, but with the hopeless finality of death.

Once, ONCE again! Her voice, a little discomforted, but always low and honeyed, steals into the midst of his temptation.

"You see, I have a pleasant aspect. I get all the morning sun. That oak just outside is full of birds and their nests. I have counted twenty-two different kinds this spring."

He has for the moment fought down the fury of his temptation.

"And you live here quite alone?"

"There are the servants, of course; not many of them, but all very kind. They would do anything for me; and I am out all day at the kennels or the stables—at one thing or another."

He knows that his brows must have contracted at this brief abstract of her life's employ, for she hastens to add:

"You know that I have an old nurse who still lives here. I assure you I am not badly looked after. Nasmyth sees to that."

"Nasmyth!" repeats he, momentarily struck by the name which, long half slumbering in his memory, had been recalled by his mother's mention of the one person who had shared her secret; "*Nasmyth!* I once had a nurse of that name!"

"I remember your telling me so in Eastshire. I have always forgotten to ask mine whether she is related to yours; it is an unusual name."

"Yes."

"You see"—with a half-shy, half-proud smile—"that I am tussling with my ignorance"—as his glance rests accidently upon a volume of Kitchin's "History of France," propped open upon the square schoolroom table, among such dissimilar companions as "The Dog," "Handley Cross," etc. "I have borrowed it from Mrs. Bevis. If you remember, you were so much shocked at my talking to you of a string of pearls that Louis XIV. had given to Diane de Poictiers? I thought I had better begin by studying French history. I do not make much of a hand of it yet, but I dare say you will help me—by and by."

She pauses slightly before the last word. His moment has come. He had meant to lead her gently down the slope to the whirlpool at the bottom. Now he must hurl her, without warning, over the precipice.

"Honor, there will be no by and by for us. That is what I have come to tell you!"

CHAPTER XIV.

This is his idea of breaking his news! The shock is so sudden, so absolutely unlooked and unprepared for, that the faintly staining blush with which she had alluded to their joint future is still lingering while a slow and apparently difficult comprehension of his words dawns upon her. Her mind always moves slowly, and among his minutes of acutest torment he afterward sets high that one in which he had stood by and seen the tardy birth in her eyes of the knowledge that he is renouncing her. She stands perfectly still in her dart-uprightness—not swaying, as his mother had done, under her blow, nor with any least indication of imminent swooning. When the understanding of his meaning has at length reached her, she even speaks:

"Your mother?"

The words, though low, are coldly clear.

"No, no; not mother! Do not think that!"

"What then?"

"She was ready—she is ready to take you to her heart. God bless her for it!"

"What then?"

To that "What then?" he knows he must respond; but though he has had two nights and days in which to frame it, he cannot bring out the answer.

The stunned astonishment of her face is stirred into life by a stab of hurt self-respect.

"It is my upbringing, then? My surroundings? You are afraid to take a wife who comes of such a stock?"

He makes a gesture of passionate negation at this most innocently cruel reversal of the truth. If she had sought intentionally in her whole armory for the weapon that would inflict on him the deepest, jaggedest wound, she could not have been more successful.

She pauses another minute, and puts her hand to her brow, as if to marshal her poor thoughts in decent order, then says with steady dignity:

"It is because you find that you do not care enough for me?"

He lets even this pass for a moment or two without contradiction, partly because in the whole storehouse of language he finds no disclaimers that are not impotently inadequate to proclaim his denial, partly because the idea flashes across his whirling brain, "Shall he leave her in her delusion?"

The one thing now to be hoped for her, in her relation to him, is that she should forget him; the one wish, that in either honor or pity he can frame for her, is that forgetfulness should come as quickly as possible; and there is nothing that would hasten its arrival so much as a belief in his unworthiness. Shrined in the sanctuary of that clean heart, no unworthy thing can long abide. But whether the lifelong habit of truthfulness is too strong, or the pain of the idea is too intolerable, it is only for a moment or two that he entertains it. Long enough, though, for her to have one superlatively bitter moment of humiliated belief in the hypothesis she has suggested.

"Because I do not care enough for you?" he says, repeating her own words, and there is that in his accent which tells her that whatever calamity is hanging over her, at least it is not that supremest one. "No, Honor, it is because—I *do* care enough." Again he halts. With his whole long black life ahead of him, he must allow himself the one white minute which the reassurance sprung into her wounded eyes gives him. *One* white moment, and then indefinite inky years! "I must give you up, because I have no right—I have never had the right—to ask *any* woman to marry me."

"Do you mean that you are poor?"

The light in her great eyes is brightening.

"No; would God it were that! We should not mind that much, should we?"

He is still—unworthily as he feels—dallying with the exquisite delight, snatched from mid agony, given him by the knowledge that she is longing to tell him that any disability he can lay upon himself will only centuple her joy in giving herself to him. And she knows what poverty is, too!—that large, straggling, big-boned poverty, which is so much harder to bear than its neat, compact six-roomed brother.

"Is there anything against you, then? Do people say anything bad about you? If they do, whatever it is, I should not believe them; and even if it *were* true——"

There is such a fire of faith, and almost protecting

valor, emanating from the whole little confident figure before him that he feels he must catch her to his heart—that heart on which, through all the veil of her perfect modesty, he discerns that she asks nothing better than to lie—unless he secures her aloofness by at once speaking out. Yes, she will be willing enough to keep her distance from him then.

"I do not know that people have anything to say against me—anything, that is, for which I am to blame; but since last we met I have made the discovery that there is a hereditary curse upon me."

Not the slightest lessening of the valorous faith in her eye. Her lip curls.

"Do you believe in curses?"

"Unfortunately, this is a case in which there is no room for disbelief—a case of hereditary disease—*madness!*" The severing word is out. There cannot be any doubt as to her having heard it, yet she draws a step nearer. "My father died in a madhouse, so did *his* father!"

His voice would naturally sink to a whisper in making this dreadful statement, but in the determination that there shall be no misapprehension he makes it almost loudly. And yet at the end of this sentence, also, she is again closer to him than before. She is drawing a long breath of relief.

"Is that all?"

"*All!* But you do not take it in. I have"—speaking very slowly and distinctly—"hereditary madness in my family—the worst kind of madness—*homicidal mania!*" Do what he will, he cannot prevent a dropping of tone at the last two words.

Her only answer is—not to *fling*, for that would imply a sudden passing impulse, but with resolved quiet to bind her arms about his neck.

"I thought that you were going to tell me something that would part us."

For one tranced moment he accepts her embrace—giving it her, indeed, wildly back. Then he loosens the warm, delicate fetters, and, stepping a pace away, holds her two hands in his, to insure himself against her in her exaltation unmanning him by a second such caress.

"You do not take it in," he says, governing his utterance, though his breath comes short: "I have homicidal madness in my blood! My father, my grandfather, other relations, died in a madhouse!"

"What are your father or your grandfather to me?"

"I am not mad *now*, but since I have the tendency in my blood, the germs may develop at any period of my life. If I were to marry you—if I were to marry *any* woman—I should be committing a crime! Do you realize"—seeing little conviction and less fear in her eyes—"that if we were man and wife I might go mad at any moment and murder you?"

"I do not think you would; but if you did"—with a slight gesture of indifference—"I have never been of much account; it would not matter." For a minute, awestruck love and wonder drive him off the lines of calm reason and demonstration he has been battling with himself to keep to, strike him dumb, and she has time to add: "And we should probably have a good spell of life together. If *I* am willing to risk it, I think *you* may."

"And you mean to say that you would not be *afraid*?"

"*Afraid!*" with an accent of lingering reflection. "No, I do not think so; I am not very apt to be afraid. I suppose it is because I have no imagination."

"And you would risk it? You love me enough to hazard putting your life into the hands of a possible—perhaps I ought to say *probable*—madman and murderer? I ought to be sorry, but, God forgive me, I can't help being glad!"

"It is a bargain, then?" she says, strongly pressing the hands that more in self-defense than in endearment, hold hers locked. "We take each other with all our drawbacks. It is but fair"—with the lightening of a solemn joy in either eye—"that they should not all be on my side."

But at that he comes to himself.

"A bargain!" he cries, starting back, and freeing his hands, not without an effort, from hers. "God forbid—yes, God forbid that I should ever fall as low as *that!* Do you suppose that, had I known, I should ever have had the villainy to entangle your life with mine? *Now* there is nothing to be done but to disentangle them—to say good-by, and to say it shortly."

The extremity of his pain has lent an almost brutal brusqueness to look and tone. But there is no quailing in the eyes that meet his. She folds the arms that he has rejected within each other and faces him.

"There must be two to that bargain. *You* may say

good-by; I never will! If you ever wanted me *really*—and you *did!*"—with a look of high confidence—"you must want me worse than ever now; and I—I want *you!* Mad or sane, I want you badly —*badly!*"

Her voice drops a little in her deep emotion, but there is no blush on her cheek. The contrast between the perfect quiet of her attitude and the concentrated passion of her words is so startling, that for a minute or two he can feel nothing but the domination of her will. If he does not make a supreme effort his own will melt before it. Duty, principle, will shrivel up like straw, in the solemn fire of those eyes.

But before he can find the strenuous words which must silence her, she goes on:

"There is no one else to whom my life or death matters. They do matter to you! You do not know"—with a touch of wistful pleading that yet does not affect the resoluteness of her whole strain—"of what use I could be to you in fighting off this horrible specter. With me on the one side and your mother on the other, do not you think you could keep it at bay?"

It is with a look of such high inspiration that she asks this question, that he feels he has no time to lose if he does not mean to let her conviction carry him away into the bottomless gulf of iniquity which an acceptance of her offer would mean.

"You must listen to me," he says, with an authority which, though it in naught lessens the mixed flame and iron of her look, yet for the moment insures obedience. "You have stated *your* side of the question; you must now let me state mine, and bring this bitter, bitter hour to an end."

"It has no bitterness for me but what you have put into it."

"Even if I had the incredible baseness to accept the sacrifice you offer me—I knew that you would offer it; I told my mother that you would!" in almost triumphant parenthesis—"there is one consideration that must have stopped me."

He paused, as if an insuperable difficulty in choosing the right words barred his utterance.

"If we had only *ourselves* to consider——"

"Whom else? I have *nobody;* I never was glad of it before. And *you*—do you mean your mother?"

For the first time there is a slight sign of trepidation in her look.

"No, no! My mother—God reward her!—had come quite round. As I told you, she is most willing to take you into her heart. My mother—oh, if you knew what she has been, what she has borne! My mother is one of the saints of God!"

"Yes, I know that; you have always told me so. I mean, I do not doubt it. But if it is not she, who or what is it?"

"Even if we had a right to do what we pleased with our own lives——"

"Well?"

"We have—no—right—to—tamper—with—lives that come after us."

The infinitely difficult words are out, and with a

colossal effort he has spoken them clearly and collectedly.

She has been awaiting them with the same exalted confidence as has characterized her whole reception of his communication—a confidence that nothing which he can utter can alter or weaken her resolution to cleave to him. But, as the meaning of his words penetrates her brain, he sees a darkening and clouding of the whole landscape of her little rapt countenance.

"You mean that we might have children?"

"Yes; children to whom I have nothing but a curse to bequeath."

She stands a moment or two, intensely thinking, her face falling, falling.

"I had not thought of that. No, that would not be fair."

She had been standing braced and tense. Now there comes a slackening and loosening, as it were, of all her powers. Her arms fall flaccidly to her side, and her eyes stare—the heavenly fire of generosity and sacrifice dead in them—straight before her.

But it is only for a moment. In a moment she is iron and fire again.

"It would not be fair to have children," she says, in a voice that, though low, is not hesitating, nor does any tinge of shamed red alter the ivory of her cheek. "But why should we have any? Are not we enough for each other?"

For a full minute stupefaction keeps him dumb; then, in a voice as unassured and uneven as hers has been even and confident, he stammers:

"You do not know what you are saying!"

"I know perfectly."

The words issue from her mouth in perfect sad simplicity. He sees that she has lost sight of all other considerations but the passionate desire to make him know that she comprehends the full scope of the sacrifice she offers.

"You think now, in the magnificence of your generosity, that it would be a small thing," he says, catching, in his dire need, some slight reflex of her absolute directness. "But think what it would be, as the years went on, to be forever tied in unescapable bondage to such a fear as anyone who shares her life with me must accept, and shut out forever from the hope of motherhood."

There is no smallest relaxing of the iron lines in her face.

"Children are but a doubtful good," she says sententiously.

"Even if I escape my doom,—it is quite possible that I may,—its shadow must always be upon my life. You *must* know that I can never again be the same man I have been."

Silence, but the silence of a rock against which the noisy waves break in sprayey futility.

"I do not myself yet realize the full bearing of what I have learned," he says, putting his hand to his head with a look of confused misery; "but I know that it is commensurate with my life—that there is no part of it which it does not affect. When I first tried to grasp it, the one thing that I could get firm hold of was this—*this*—that I have come here to-day for. You must understand that it was not I who asked you to marry me at The Beeches. I should never have been such a scoundrel——"

"It was you who asked me!" She takes away speech from his stammering lips. "Have you forgotten so soon? You said to me, 'Hast thou any mind of me?' And I answered, 'I have even great mind of thee.' I never spoke a truer word in my life. *I have even great mind of thee.*"

She tenders no caress such as would match the absolute surrender of her words, such as earlier she had innocently offered; but her eyes, which with their dilated pupils seem to occupy almost the whole of her small face, scorch his very soul with the intolerable fervor of their love and prayer. He clasps his hands before his own eyes, and behind them he, too, prays, but it is to God to help him in this horrible temptation. Then, dropping them again with as sudden and violent a gesture, he gasps out, "Will you make me mad before my time?" and is gone.

. . . . .

The Bramshill family make up for their delay in returning to London after Whitsun by staying to the bitter end, when once they go thither. The late season has shown more appreciation of Euphemia than the early one, or, at all events, brought her more balls. Those festivities, indeed, have in latter times shown a tendency to become huddled into the end of July; filial and conjugal piety keeps the wives and daughters of ill-starred members of the English legislature lingering on even well into August. But it is now time to be gone, as the smell of the wood pavement and its throaty dust plainly proclaim.

Miss Bramshill lies exhausted, after a terrific day of accumulated sultry gayeties, planning rural joys.

"It is very odd that we have never met Harry Clarence anywhere this season. How glad I shall be to see him again!"

To her surprise her mother does not "rise," and the spirit of mischief prompts her to try the effect of a stronger expression of approval.

"After all, what a different feeling one has to a real *bonâ fide* man like him from what those little decadent boys who 'bunch' one"—with an ungrateful glance toward the floral tributes with which the room is filled—"inspire one! I shall send for him as an antiseptic."

This last speech does produce an effect, though not the one expected. Lady Bramshill hurries to the window, wide flung to the smutty London night air, and leans out, panting.

"You *may* send," she says ominously.

Euphemia is lying on her bed, too tired even to begin to undress; but this enigmatic sentence brings her instantaneously into a sitting posture.

"What do you mean? I *may send?* Of course I may."

"I mean"—in an extremely troubled voice—"that however much you may send for him, you will not get him."

In a second Euphemia's long tired legs, no longer conscious of fatigue, are flung over the bedside, and she has raced to her parent in the window.

"Have you forbidden him the house? I remember now that since that mysterious interview you had with him in June, he never came near us. I cannot understand what you could have to say to him that needed such privacy. Oh, if you have, *what* a mess you have made of it!"

She has poured out her words in fiery haste, and having reached her parent, lays a compelling hand upon her shoulder, the moral if not the physical force of which obliges her to turn round a disturbed and guilty countenance.

"I did it for the best."

"You did *what* for the best?"

"Whatever I did, I did kindly; for his mother's sake, I was sure to do it quite kindly."

"*What* did you do quite kindly?"

Silence.

"Did you forbid him the house quite kindly?"

"Whatever I did, I did it for the best—for *your* sake."

"For *my* sake?"

"I thought—apparently I was wrong, but one can only judge by appearances—that, unconsciously, without any dishonorable intention, he was growing fonder of you than he had any right to be."

"*Any right to be?* Why, in Heaven's name, should not he be fond of me if he chose? Oh, if you would but allow me to manage my own affairs!"

"He has no right to be fond of anyone, poor fellow! and I thought he knew it, but it seems he did not."

"Did not know what?" cries Euphemia, in a key

of the most exasperated bewilderment. "Once or twice before you have thrown out dark hints about his past. What has he done? Has he cheated at cards? I do not know anything else that a man may not do with impunity; but you would not have had him at the house if he had done that. What *has* he done?"

"He has not done anything that I know of, poor fellow!"

The girl gives utterance to an inarticulate expression of excessive impatience; then, as though a sudden light of comprehension had lit up her intelligence, she adds quickly:

"Is it because his father was a drunkard? As if most people's fathers,"—scornfully,—"and *all* their grandfathers, had not drunk more than they ought."

"He was not a drunkard that I know of: he was"—seeing that she can no longer shirk the telling of that ugly tale, whose last utterance had been so painful—"he was, since you must know, a raving maniac. He died in a madhouse; so did *his* father. They have it—homicidal mania—in their family."

There is a minute's silence. The healthy roses, which not even the burning of the midnight electric light had chased from the girl's face, have disappeared ere she speaks again.

"*And you told him of it?*"

"I thought he knew."

"You told him because you imagined that he was in love with me?"

"Yes."

"If I had had but an inkling of it! He who hates

big women! who detests girls that speak disrespectfully to their parents! who only tolerated me because I talked to him of Honor!"

"*Honor!* Do you mean to say that it was Honor whom he was in love with?"

"Of course I do; anybody but a *bat* could have seen it."

"*Honor!*" repeats Lady Bramshill, in a tone of almost stupefaction; "that little black thing! and when *you* were by!"

The inveteracy of the mother's pride, overstepping even her real concern at the mischief she has done, gives a second of mollified amusement to her daughter.

"I know that you meant it for the best; but, oh, you *have* made a mess of it!"

Lady Bramshill turns away, and begins to walk up and down the room.

"I wish to Heaven now that I had kept clear of them!"

"I am sure so do they, poor souls!"

"But, after all"—in uneasy self-justification—"it was a most natural mistake, and one that you yourself did everything to foster."

"Yes, I did. I wish to Heaven I had not. I thought it such a good joke."

"And its being Honor instead of you makes no real difference; a motherless girl in my charge——"

"At the present moment mothers do not seem to me such an unmixed blessing," replies Euphemia, in a tone of deep irritation.

Then, seeing with some slight remorse, which yet

breeds a still deeper vexation, the hurt look on her parent's large face, which gives an ample area for the play of her feelings, she goes on :

"I know that you meant well ; but for the future commend me to people who mean ill. If you had not told him, nobody else would : and he and Honor would have gone on to the end of the chapter in happy ignorance, and as sane as the rest of us—saner than some."

Lady Bramshill does what she has been thinking of doing since the beginning of the conversation, and bursts into tears.

"I am sure I did it for the best," she says between sobs suited to her size—"so fond as I have always been of Lucy—far more so than she has ever seemed of me—and of him, too, poor fellow ! I always stood up for him when you called him a prig."

"It is nearly a year since I called him a prig."

"She ought to have told him—Lucy ought to have told him."

"I differ from you entirely ; I think she was perfectly right. If he knew that he was liable to such a disease, he was far more likely to develop it. *Now* he will probably be in a madhouse in six months."

Lady Bramshill stops sobbing, and stares in consternation at her daughter. It is evident that this is a view of the subject which has never before presented itself to her.

"He *looks* so thoroughly sane," pursues the girl thoughtfully. "Did his father look sane ? Is he at all like him ?—in person, I mean."

"Not in the least. His father was a small, dark

man with a big head. No, Harry is *quite* unlike him."

"A small, dark maniac with a big head!" repeats Euphemia, in a tone of the profoundest compassion. "*Poor* Mrs. Clarence!"

"He has not a *look* of his father. If Lucy were not such a saint, one might really have thought"—then, pulling herself up—"I do not know what one might not have thought——"

But though Lady Bramshill leaves her speculation unexplained, her daughter has not been born in the end of the nineteenth century for nothing, and she is able to carry out her mother's unspoken reasoning without much difficulty.

"Was she *always* such a saint!"

"Always—*always.*"

CHAPTER XV.

Mrs. Clarence has need of all her saintliness when her son comes back to tell her by his looks—he is much too generous to do it in words—that she need never again shoot her little arrows of disparagement at the woman he loves. The "little black woman," whose supposed likeness to herself she has so resented, and all other women, black and fair, are cleared out of her path. Her boy is hers, and hers alone, for life.

She never asks, and he never volunteers, the details of the parting interview. She only knows that he returns to her on the night but one after it—he never explains where he had passed the intervening night, but, from the haggard dishevelment of his appearance, she feels sure that it must have been out of doors—returns to her with ten years added to his face; returns to sit on his low stool and lay his head on her knee.

Neither of them sheds a tear, or alludes even obliquely to the cataclysm that has washed away the son's future. The nearest approach made by either to the subject on that first night is when he lifts his head, after an hour of absolute silence, and asks:

"You are not very much attached to this place? You would not mind leaving it?"

Her answer is to repeat his words in a dreadful

voice, in which his ear recognizes an anguish superior even to his own :

"*Attached to this place! Mind leaving it!*"

In a week they are gone, leaving the house in the agents' hands, and with no trace of their sojourn beyond an address at the post office, and a stab of remorse in Lady Bramshill's breast as often—which is no oftener than she can possibly help—as she drives down the little grass-grown *cul-de-sac* whence she had been so resolute to updig her girlhood's friend.

They go—the son and the mother. He takes rooms for them both in a farmhouse accustomed to let summer lodgings, and with a certain homely comfort in its arrangements, in that heavenly country which combines the highest cultivation with a rural wildness of heath and hillside—the Surrey of Guildford and Godalming, of Dorking and Shere.

Since no one of their acquaintance knows of their neighborhood, Mrs. Clarence will not be tormented by the trivialities of visiting, and yet—so peopled is the sweet solitude—she will not feel lonely ; and her son has an even shorter distance to traverse in order to run down to her from London than he had at St. Gratian.

She acquiesces in all his provisions for her comfort, not with the old soft pliancy to his will, but with a numbness of indifference that disquiets him. Sometimes the idea strikes him, with a painful oddness, that, though it is himself whom the blow has struck, it is *she* who is felled by it. Can mother-love further go ?

Often, on his return, he finds that she has not been

out of doors at all, but has lain, day-long, in her chair at the window, looking out on the stretch of heather which advances its ever-more-purpling sea of bloom to the very doors. Sometimes, on the other hand, he comes back to find her exhausted with restless ramblings for many hours,—ramblings beyond her strength,—and from which she returns empty-handed, not having had—how unlike her old self!—the spirit to pull one of the innumerous gay blossoms which the chalk formation of the Hog's Back sends up so plentifully along its multicolored ridges.

It is, perhaps, good for her son that puzzled care for her state distracts him in some measure from the monotony of his own ruin.

One night, after their simple dinner, as he sits beside her in the unlighted room—unlighted save by the silver sword of a penetrating full moon—he takes her tenderly to task.

"Dearest!" he says—of late he has used many more fond words to her than he was wont to employ, but they bring no light into her face—"dearest, you must not let yourself be so knocked down." He pauses; then goes on, "You knew it all along."

He feels her little feverish fingers stir in his, as if she would withdraw them.

"Yes, yes."

Her agitation is so obvious, even through the strong effort of her suppression, that he feels he must at once change the subject:

"Are you getting tired of this place?"

"No, it does very well."

"It is certainly very peaceful!" looking out on

the silent common, out of which the moon has sucked all its amethyst, substituting her own argent.

"Yes, very peaceful."

"And your church? Do you like it? Are there enough services? and is the doctrine to your mind?"

She hesitates palpably.

"I have no doubt that the services are very nice, but I have not been there yet."

He stares at her in ungovernable astonishment, the remembrance flashing upon him for the first time that on the one or two Sundays he has spent with her she has happened to be too languid and ill after a sleepless night to leave her window-chair. But he had attributed the omission wholly to accident, and now learns with amazement that it had been due to deliberate intention. She, who, like Malcolm's mother,

> "Oftener upon her knees than on her feet,"
> Died every day she lived"—

whose ardor of daily worship has often injured her health—can it be that she has abandoned those practices of devotion which, as long as he can remember, have been the mainspring and backbone of her life? His own faith is of a slack and dubious kind; but what a precious possession hers has been to him he only now learns by the shock he receives at the implication her words carry of having loosened her hold upon it.

At the blank astonishment in his face a slight quiver passes over hers.

"Shall we take a turn on the heath?" she asks;

"It is really, without any figure of speech, quite as light as day."

And he knows that this subject, too, is closed.

. . . . .

"Nana," says Honor Lisle, addressing her former nurse by the old childish title whose liquids appear —judging by their universality—to be the easiest form of utterance to a baby mouth, "did you ever live with a family of the name of Clarence?"

Mrs. Nasmyth is in the act of leaving the room— Honor's paintless schoolroom boudoir,—but thus addressed pauses, and looks over her shoulder.

"Yes, I did."

"I wonder you never mentioned them to me."

"I am not one for talking much; but why do you ask?"

"Because I wanted to know."

The direct answer is enough, but apparently does not seem exhaustive to the questioner, for she shuts the door, and returns into the room:

"Have you heard anything about them? Are they alive still? Have you been meeting Mrs. Clarence?"

"Yes, I have met her."

"And Master Harry? Why he must be a man of near thirty by now! Have you met him, too?"

"Yes."

Her manner is studied in its colorlessness; but either it is overstudied, or a lifelong acquaintance with her has made the servant familiar with her modes of veiling emotion, for she looks hard at her.

"And I that have never seen him since he was five

years old—dear little man! How he cried when I left! 'Don't go, Nana, don't go!' I can hear him now, and I never would have left him of my own accord! I have never seen him since he was five years old, unless——"

"Unless what?"

"Unless"—with a still keener look at the half-averted face—"unless that was he—the gentleman who came to call on you so early one day last week. I saw him from the workroom window as he was going away. He turned and gave one look up at the house."

"Yes, that was Mr. Clarence."

"It *was* really?" with a great accession of interest; "that really *was* Master Harry? Dear me! what a fine-looking gentleman he has grown! But he always *was* a grand boy! Such an appetite! Such a pair of legs! So *that* was Master Harry? Ah, then"—more to herself than to Honor—"that accounts for it!"

"Accounts for what?"

But Mrs. Nasmyth is silent, apparently lost in retrospect. Honor's turned-away face has inevitably veered round.

"You cannot mean that you recognized him after all those years?"

"Recognized him! Oh, no! Why, he was only five years old when I left him!"

"Then what do you mean by saying, 'That accounts for it'?"

"You must not take one up so sharp, Miss Honor. I do not know that I meant anything very particular."

"I suppose you mean that you detected a likeness in him to his father. You certainly could not find one to his mother."

"No; he never had a look of her. It used to make her mad that he had not."

"Then"—with a sinking heart—"he is like his father—like Mr. Clarence?"

One would have thought that to such a query the "Yes" or "No" would come easily, and without delay; but Mrs. Nasmyth hesitates, and her answer, when she utters one, is oblique:

"Mr. Clarence was not much to look at."

"You mean that his son is a handsome likeness of him?"

"No, I do not."

"Then"—rising from her window seat, and going close up to her nurse in undefined yet strong excitement—"then what *do* you mean?"

The intensity of asking in her somber eyes would seem as if it must force out a reply, but none comes.

"What did you mean by saying, 'That account for it'?"

"As I told you,"—looking uneasily doorward, a glance to which the girl rejoins by placing herself between her companion and the exit,—"I do not know that I mean anything particular; it slipped out."

"*What* slipped out?"

Her strong small hands are gripping her nurse's wrists, and the current of her will is passed through them and through her eyes into the other's being.

"Indeed, Miss Honor, you have no right to press me like this—just for a chance word, too. But, since you *will* have it, you know as well as I that people's *real* fathers are not always those that give them their names."

There is a dead silence—so dead that the light noise made by one of the many finches in the oak tree outside, springing from twig to twig, is distinctly audible.

For the first moment the meaning of her companion's words fails to reach Miss Lisle's brain; then, as its ugly import passes into that clean little sanctuary, she drops Mrs. Nasmyth's hands, and rather falls than steps a pace backward.

"There, now! you would have it, and I knew you would not like it. It is not a pretty thing to tell a young lady; but then you are not like other young ladies."

Still total silence.

"I wish that you would not look at me like that, Miss Honor. It is not *my* fault. You *would* have it; and you have no one to thank but yourself."

The moral shocks that make milestones in our lives are not, like the physical ones, always accompanied by appropriate action. After that first falling back, Honor betrays by no gesture that she has reached one of life's turning-points; only her eyes, like gimlets, drill holes in her companion's face.

"You have gone mad!" she says, in a very low and perfectly controlled voice. "Do you know what you are implying?"

"I do not know what you mean, Miss Honor, by 'implying,'" replies the other, wincing, not unnaturally, under the girl's terrible pointblankness. "As

I stand here, I am telling you nothing but the truth. I should not have told any other young lady ; but you are used to hearing such things talked about. And, indeed, I should not have told you if you had not forced it out of me. I am sure"—half whimpering—"I have no wish to hurt the poor lady, though she did not behave altogether very handsome by me. I have never even mentioned the family to you in all these years—have I, now ?"

The question goes unanswered. The girl stands stock-still, with the live coals of her eyes still burning, *burning* into the servant, while within her an earthquake seems shaking all her few and strong beliefs.

Honor has no great cause to love Mrs. Clarence ; but yet, seen through her son's eyes, she has—since first the girl knew that son—stood to her as the embodiment of that purity and godliness which, in her own life-circle, she has known only by their absence. If this hideous imputation be true, chastity, piety themselves, must have gone by the board, or have never existed at all save in the brains of idle dreamers.

"It is a lie !" she says, with steady concentration. "You must be a very wicked woman to have invented such a black one. The lady you speak of is one of the saints of God !"

Unconsciously she has caught at the plank which the phrase she has so often heard Harry use with regard to his mother offers her: "*One of the saints of God!*" So associated is the term in her mind with the pure-faced, holy-eyed widow, that at the word "saint" the image of Mrs. Clarence rises much more readily before her mental vision than does any of the sweet canonized figures that enrich the Church's page.

"I am sure I do not know about that," returns the other doggedly. "I dare say she may be *now ;* and I am sure, poor thing! I do not want to make her out worse than she was. If ever anyone had an excuse, it was she. Dear me! she was a nice young lady when I first went to live with her—just sixteen! It would be impossible to see a handsomer couple than they made."

"Than *who* made?"

"She was engaged to her cousin, a young gentleman in the navy."

"And married him?"

"Her guardian would not hear of it—she had no father or mother alive. He was a having sort of man, and I believe he thought that if she married a poor man she would be always coming back upon his hands, and so he broke it off. And not long after Mr. Clarence offered; and what with their badgering her,—the guardian and his wife, I mean,—and her own spirit being so broken that she did not much care what became of her, she ended by taking him. Of course, she did not know a syllable about the madness. They took good care to keep *that* from her."

There is a pause. Honor's nostrils are inflated, and her hands clenched. Self-controlled as she habitually is, it is a long moment before she can be sure enough of her voice to command the key in which she must speak her next sentence.

"I suppose that, so far, what you have just told

me is true; there is no reason why you should have invented it. What you implied before is *not* true, and I do *not* believe it; but since you have brought such an accusation against a lady who never had a wicked thought in her life, I shall not allow you to leave the room until you have told me on what grounds you founded it."

The old servant bursts into tears.

"Indeed, Miss Honor, I do not know what has come to you! You never spoke to me like that in all these years! and I am sure it is not my fault. How can I help it if ladies will—— But there, I shall make you angry again! You had better let me go, and think no more about it."

"You must tell me, please, at once."

Something in the tone of the austere young judge before her—that something which, from the time that she was five years old, her nurse has recognized as not to be resisted whenever, rarely enough, it has appeared—tells Mrs. Nasmyth that her tears and resistances are vain, and with one more protesting "Well, it is not my fault; you may believe it or not, as you choose," she goes on:

"They had been married not quite six months when the secret—about the madness, I mean—came out. Mr. Clarence had a slight attack; and when she found out what sort of life she was in for, she nearly went mad herself, poor lady! She was ill for weeks; and when she was convalescent the doctor sent her away to the seaside, to get up her strength —and, of course, I went with her. We went to Southsea."

Again a pause.

"Well?"

"It happened that the *Invincible*, her cousin's ship, had just come into Portsmouth, and when she and I were walking on the Green one day we met him face to face."

"Yes."

"She was very lonely, poor thing! She had no acquaintances at Southsea, and she was only seventeen and a half."

"Yes!" still in that voice of severe brevity which, while admitting no belief in the told tale, yet insists on its continuance.

"She always had been dotingly fond of him since she was a baby, and they had belonged to one another, in a way, poor things!"

"Well?"

"He came every day after that. I began to get frightened at last; but it was not any good, they had quite lost their heads."

Again the narrator stops, but is not as immediately as before driven on by the listener to a resumption of the story. The very unwillingness with which that story is torn piecemeal from the teller's lips—her evident want of animus against the subjects of it—her, on the contrary, obvious inclination to palliate their offense—is breeding in the girl's mind a reluctant creeping belief in the tale; and it is with a less assured accent of incredulity that she puts the question:

"And Mr. Clarence—was he mad all the while?"

"Oh, dear no! it had only been quite a slight attack, just a threatening—nobody knew anything about it but she and I; he was recovered long before *she* was. He came to see her once or twice at Southsea, but she would not have anything to say to him. She was quite gentle,—she never could be anything else,—and she did not reproach him at all, but she could not forgive him for having deceived her." After a slight pause: "That was in the summer, and next spring Master Harry was born."

There is a matter-of-factness in the statement of this last event, uttered in a rather lowered but perfectly confident voice, which makes the crawling belief against which she has been struggling writhe itself yet a step further into Honor's heart. Her knees seem melting beneath her; but since to sit down or make any change in her attitude would be a confession of effect produced by that narrative, the hearing of which she had prefaced by so passionate an expression of disbelief, she keeps her former standing position, and, though objects swim before her eyes, she refrains from even lifting a hand to clear away the blur. But it is beyond her to speak at once, and for a minute or two the only sound audible is that of a caged goldfinch sharpening his beak agains this perch.

After that interval, dimly feeling through the chaos of as yet unrealized emotion that is surging within her that silence itself is acquiescence, she compels her lips to utterance:

"Was Mr. Clarence in his right mind at the time of the boy's birth?"

"Oh, yes, as sane as you or I."

"And you wish me to believe that he accepted the child as his son?"

"Indeed, Miss Honor, I do not wish you to believe anything of the sort. I only tell you just what happened. Mr. Clarence never took the least notice of the child. People have often passed the remark to me how odd it was that he did not, and Master Harry such a beautiful infant, too!"

"Though he was perfectly sane at the time, he accepted the disgrace quite calmly—is that what I am to credit?"

The scorn in her tone is, perhaps, the more accentuated for the lurking faltering that underlies it.

"As I have told you, miss, he never took the least notice of the child; but I suppose in a way he 'accepted' it, as you call it, since he forgave her."

"*Forgave her!*"

The incredulity—a little forced in the last sentence—is genuine enough now.

"I do not know about forgiving her really, but he let her live on in the same house with him. She no doubt told him the whole story from beginning to end,—by the time we left Southsea she was quite desperate,—and he—he was not a bad-hearted man when he was in his right wits—and he knew that he had done her a great wrong in marrying her, and she was not much more than a child, and so altogether—— But he never would look at Master Harry!" She stops, as if relieved at having ended an unpleasant task; but the unbroken silence which follows apparently disposes her to add a rider: "She was very grateful to him, poor soul! I will say that for her. That was why she never—till the last half year, when he got beyond her or anybody—would have him shut up during his attacks. Like many mad people, he had a horror, when he was sane, of being put in a madhouse. She did not seem to mind how much he knocked her about, nor whether he killed her or not. For months together she carried her life in her hand,— such a little delicate thing as she looked,—but I have never met her equal for spirit—*never!* If she had not been so jealous of me about Master Harry,—she could not bear to think that he cared for anyone in the world but her,—we should never have parted."

The goldfinch is washing now. How plainly in the stillness the tiny squirt of water over his back and the shaking of his feathers is heard! The voice that breaks upon his bathing is so low as not to drown its little noises.

"I have listened to your story, but you must not think that that means I have believed it. You have given absolutely *no* proof of what you have asserted."

"I do not want anybody to believe it," replies the servant again, half crying. "I had far rather have said nothing about it; only you would have it out of me. What can it matter to anyone now whether it is true or not? Mr. Clarence has been dead five-and-twenty years, and the other gentleman went down with all hands in a gunboat he commanded somewhere Newfoundland way six months before, and Mrs. Clarence has turned into a sort of saint, you say. I am not in the least suprised at *that*, for through it all she was a very religious-feeling kind of woman; and Mr. Harry will never know a syllable about it, so what difference *can* it make to anyone whether it is true or not?"

"*What difference can it make to anyone whether it is true or not?*"

As the words pass Mrs. Nasmyth's lips the answer to them flashes in a sea of scorching light into Honor's mind. If the tale be true, there is no obstacle between her and Harry.

CHAPTER XVI.

"THE judge does not seem to have had a bad journey," says Euphemia Bramshill, looking through a letter which has reached her by one of those afternoon posts, which now, blessing us in the depth of the rural districts, almost reconcile one to living in the nineteenth century. "Hamburg is very full. The prince arrived; the Empress Frederick expected. He has made acquaintance with the woman who wrote 'Cesspools.' It seems she published them to support a sick husband. She seems to be a good deal lionized. Ah, how unfortunate! He crossed in the same boat with your victim, Harry Clarence. How that poor fellow must hate the sight of any of us!"

"Does the judge say how he was looking?" asks Lady Bramshill, in that voice of thorough discomfiture with which she now alludes—as seldom as possible—to the Clarence family. "But no, he never notices anything; and, besides, he does not know that there is any reason for alteration. Was she—was his mother with him?"

"Father does not mention her."

"That is strange. She told me that they always made their little trips together."

"I should think she was probably dead," rejoins

Euphemia, with purposed brutality. "She always looked as if she had not much of a grip upon life."

The remark drives her mother out of the room; but it is not true. Mrs. Clarence is not dead. She is still at her Surrey farmhouse; but now, in this September weather, she is alone there. The vacation has sent the whole machinery of the law steaming and yachting and training over the face of Europe, and has filled one member of the bar, who has not yet taken flight, with an inexpressible longing to be away, too. He has the reverse of Ritter Toggenburg's impulse, who found solace in building a hut close to the cloister that held his lost lady, and dedicated his life to watching for the opening of her casement and the daily glimpse of her unattainable nun's face.

Clarence, on the contrary, feels that if he could step off into another planet he would have a better chance of getting the ring of his love's passionately begging little voice out of his ears, the look of her anguish-dilated pupils out of his eyes. The absolute silence in which humanity toward his mother makes him endure his torments; the hideous complication of suffering in the total loss of all hope of attaining the one thing he had ever ardently desired, coupled with the dread of the awful overhanging doom revealed to him so late in life that its terror is in no degree blunted by custom; coupled, too, with the need of feigning impossible cheerfulness in the endeavor to lift Mrs. Clarence's prostrated spirits, combine to make a situation which by and by he has to acknowledge to himself is beyond his power of bearing.

Once or twice a ripple of indignant bitterness against the companion of his wretchedness agitates the surface of his torn mind. Ought not she at least to make some effort over herself in order to try and alleviate a woe which must be so much acuter than her own? But as often as these upbraidings have occurred to him, she seems to have read his thoughts, and to force herself to some piteous efforts at gayety—efforts so piteous that he prays for the return of her unvarnished melancholy.

The strain upon his mind begins to tell upon his body, destroying appetite and undermining sleep. Instead of quiet slumber, horrid visions begin to assault his bed. Defer as he may to a later and later hour each night his going to what is no longer rest, he cannot dodge them. They are patient, and await him, even till after dawn has broken.

Nor can he better his case by resolutely lying awake; for of late odd shapes have begun to dance and curve and writhe in the dark before him. The cold drops of sweat break out on his forehead as he tells himself that it is what he must expect, that he is coming into his inheritance, that he is beginning to go mad. It is in vain that he scourges himself mentally for his want of pluck, his failure to turn with manly resolution upon the horrible specter that dogs him. The nature of the peril sets that ordinary pluck with which most educated British men are pretty well furnished at defiance, and the armor that will defend him against it is not yet forged.

By the arrival of September it is clear to him that

his one chance of escape from an entire breakdown of the nerve system is in flight.

It is with misgiving as to the light in which his mother may regard a proposition which in her normal state she would hail with joy that he makes it.

"This time last year we were off to the Loire. When we are to go *this* year?"

She is sitting listlessly sewing at one of those fine embroideries whose execution used to give her so much still pleasure, but which his eye still tells him, by its lack of progress, is only taken up in his presence. Her work falls into her lap, and from the force of old habit a ray of expectant pleasure darts into her eyes. But that it is due only to habit is evidenced by its immediate extinction in a darkness deeper than what had preceded it.

"One must be in very good repair to live in one's boxes," she says.

His spirit sinks. Is it possible that she, whose heart has always answered to each pulse of his with such almost miraculous accuracy of understanding, does not now comprehend the bitter need for change— for escape—that is corroding his whole being?

He strokes her languid arm with one of his gentlest caresses.

"It would, perhaps, be an effort to you at first, dear; but it would do us both good."

She does not answer save by a restless turning of her profile—a very sharpened outline, as not for the first time he notices—toward the now somewhat waning heather.

"You will never live to be an old woman," he

says, with a mixture of intolerable irritation and yet more intolerable remorse for feeling it, in the presence of this shadowy epitome of suffering, "if you take other people's sufferings so much to heart."

"*Other people's!*"

The bottomless depth of tragedy and—is it reproach?—it must be, though it looks like self-reproach—in her voice startles even her son, used as he now is to what had at first seemed to him the unaccountable, and, as it were, exaggerated deeps of her depression.

"I am afraid, indeed, that in this case we have all things in common," he answers, with a rueful fondness; "but it will be doing me a left-handed sort of kindness to worry yourself into your grave over my troubles. What should I do if you were dead, I should like to know?"

Perhaps it is that this letting himself go of a person whose love has always been of the unexpansive, unprotesting sort brings home afresh to his mother the shock that his whole moral nature has received; but her answer is a little low cry.

"It would be immeasurably the best thing that could happen to you!"

"I do not *quite* know how you make that out," he answers, dismayed and startled, and regaining his self-control. "However unhappy we are, we need not let ourselves say this kind of thing; we only cut each other deeper. One would think, mother, that you had been the author of my misfortunes instead of a fellow-victim."

He gives a melancholy smile at the absurdity of

the suggestion; but she only turns away again with a slight and, to him, incomprehensible shudder.

He has desisted in discouragement from any further effort to persuade her to try to relieve their wretchedness by a change of scene, but on the same evening she herself resumes the subject.

"I should have been only a clog upon you," she says, breaking abruptly into the dropped theme. "There is nothing more uncomfortable than traveling with a person who is just not up to the mark; and I am rather run down. Where shall you go?"

"*Go!* And leave you here?"

"Why not?" she asks, with that air of manufactured lightness which always hurts him more than any other of her moods. "Since the time you first went to school, I have been used to being alone all day. It is only the evenings; and I shall shorten them by going to bed early and getting my beauty sleep."

But he looks at her so ruefully that her airy tone falters away.

"It is the first time in our lives that I have ever said it or thought it," she murmurs, brokenly at first, but then steadily, "but we shall be better apart for a little while."

"Do you really think so?"

In the depth of his consciousness he recognizes that she speaks truth; but yet his heart is so sore that the idea that the one treasure left to him can do without him seems to add a new raw to his wounds.

"We hurt each other more than anyone else can hurt us," she goes on. "You said almost the same thing yourself a short while ago—did not you? If you took me abroad with you, though we went to Central Africa, it would be no change of scene. When I told you this morning that I could not go with you because I was run down, I did not speak the truth. I do not go because my sharing it with you would deprive you of any good you might gain from the trip. And, besides "—holding up a hand to stop him as she sees that he is about to interrupt her—" I *wish* to be alone."

Into her voice, so faint and faltering, now there has come a note of resolution and authority that only once or twice before in his life has he heard. It fills him with a sort of fear.

"If you *wish* to be alone, there is no more to be said."

Two days afterward he leaves her. Their parting is almost wordless; but she comes out to the farm gate to see the last of him. The road runs straight for half a mile or more across the common, and he stares till his eyes ache at the little shadowy figure that is first his dear mother, then diaphanous gray draperies, then a tiny pale blur against the sky, then nothing. But her faint "God bless you!" is never a blur, or nothing.

. . . . .

The sudden shock of the deduction drawn from Mrs. Nasmyth's tale has, for the moment, the effect upon Honor of a hard physical blow on the head, and makes her for a little space unconscious of her surroundings.

She does not actually swoon or fall down, but she

knows nothing about anything until she wakes to the fact that her nurse is standing beside her with a glass of water in her hand, and saying, in a half-self-reproachful, half-upbraiding voice :

"I ought not to have told you, but you would make me, and how could I know that you would take it so much to heart?"

"I do not want any water," answers the girl, coming, rather hazily still, out of her clouds, but with the immediate impulse to clutch at and recover her lost self-control ; "I do not know why you are offering it to me, and as to taking your tale to heart, one need not take to heart what one does not believe."

But to her own spirit she holds a different language when she has at length gained the supremely coveted boon of being alone with it. The story is, as she had pointed out to the teller, unsupported by any evidence beyond a probably imagined physical likeness. It rests solely on the testimony of a discharged servant. It is antecedently incredible—in flagrant contradiction with the whole tenor of life, the ermine purity and continuous holiness of the person of whom it is told. It is a lie, a slander, a calumny upon the face of it ; a lie so coarse, a slander so black, a calumny so villainous, that its mere statement is its refutation—and yet it is true !

The conviction that it is so does not come piecemeal and by degrees to Honor's mind, built up out of tiny mosaics of evidence, such as Mrs. Clarence's terrified avoidance of society, the very excess of her church-going, since the greatest sinners proverbially make the greatest saints ; such as the unwillingness of the witness against her, the friendly feeling obviously still surviving in that witness' mind ; not out of all these fragments, as I say, is conviction gradually built up. It comes in one blinding flash— a flash that for the moment takes away the senses of the struck. It is true, *true*, TRUE !

The burden of the revelation is too heavy to be borne indoors, particularly by one to whom a roof is always, if a needful, yet an irksome covering ; so as soon as she can rid herself of Mrs. Nasmyth's frightened assiduities, Honor slips out by a side door into the neglected park, where, hiding herself from every unlikely eye in a copse, which, shared with squirrels, had been a playground of her lonely childhood, she sits down on the fallen and never removed arm of an oak tree, blown down in some former storm, and sets herself to face the tempest—mightier than that which had felled her resting-place—raging in her mind. It is made up of such widely diverse and madly jarring elements that at first it is nothing but a frantic whirlwind, in which she can distinguish nothing clear. But by little and little the hurricane begins to resolve itself into its component parts—the original horror of shrinking disbelief, the shock of conviction, and, underlying both, a stratum of deep and, as it seems to herself, enormously wicked joy.

Joy! for if this tale be true—and it *is* true—there is no longer any ugly specter thrusting itself between her and her love ! There never has been one ! He need never have come, with his white face, to tell her that grisly tale, which has as little relation to him as to herself. If he were now in this quiet copse, he might push through the brushwood to her—might take her in his arms, and lift her to the heaven of his heart, without God or man having any right to gainsay it.

She smiles; and in the height of the blessed illusion stretches out her own arms, crying: "Come! come!"

But the sound of her voice breaks the charm. The ecstatic cry dies into silence, and the arms fall listless to her sides. Of what use is it to either of them that there is no least obstacle between them if one of them must go through life believing that a frightful demon is forever waving them apart? And who is to undeceive him? If anyone did him that service, would he survive it? In a deluge of most bitter recollections there come pouring over her memory the numberless indications which her acquaintance with him has afforded of his passionate cult for his mother—remembrance of her own jealousy at the high apartness from all other women in which he has set her—of her own despair of ever nearing the lofty throne on which, in the aloofness of her supreme purity and piety, she reigns in his heart. There are illusions which, though they be illusions, yet are of so stout a quality that with their extinction is coincident the extinction, moral or physical, and sometimes both, of those who cherish them.

He would never believe the story; and whose task could it be to force conviction on him? But if he did, the knowledge would kill him. Better—immeasurably better—for him that he should walk through life dogged by the specter of hereditary madness than that he should ever learn by what means he has been freed from it.

As the hopeless misery of the dilemma comes home to her,—she does not realize it at once,—she slips off the tree trunk, and lies along upon the matted undergrowth, with her cheek resting against the lichened bark. The roughness of the fiber irritates her soft skin, but she is too absolutely overthrown to care, or make the slight movement necessary for removing the discomfort. Though there had been no one before whom to exercise self-control, she had tried to keep a brave front to the overthrow of her happiness—tried, from the force of habit and the inherent enduring strength of her character; but this new blow—this knowledge that her calamity is all needless, in vain, wholly oversets her. It is not God-sent! It is the outcome of human wickedness.

To do her justice, it is not the enormity of her own loss that crushes her nearly so much as the agony of her pity for him—a pity that swallows up even mighty love—the measureless compassion for one doomed to stagger through life under the overwhelming weight of a burden from which he can be freed only by the imposition of a yet more intolerable one. That weight seems pressing on her own head, and she lifts herself into a sitting posture and puts her hands on the top of it.

"It would be a good thing if I could cry, I suppose," she says out loud; but the refreshment of tears is leagues away.

The change of posture seems to bring another aspect of the subject to her mind. *His mother!* It is her colossal selfishness that, in order to shield her own early frailty, is dooming him to this lifelong hell. *His mother!* That shrine of austere purity! that ermine! that snowdrop! that saint! *His mother!* who had shrunk with such repulsion from the girl because she had mentioned Poppy de Vere! She laughs out loud; but the noise of her own grisly mirth frightens her, and she looks round scared, as if expecting to see some ill spirit that had uttered it.

Her thought takes a slightly different, but not less bitter road. *One of the saints of God!* The phrase, so often repeated to her, comes dinning back, and back, and back. Well, some of God's great saints had been great sinners in their day; but had any of them ever sought to cover their sins by so monstrous and murderous a deception?

There flashes grotesquely before her mind's eye the image of King David setting Uriah in the forefront of the battle. But even that treachery pales before the iniquity of this one. It is her own son, the son of her devotion to whom she has made a lifelong parade,—the ludicrous inaptness of the word to any action of Mrs. Clarence's does not strike the girl in her state of tension,—whom she has unhesitatingly sacrificed to her own good name. Surely at the Last Assize, when our Judge weighs our offenses, that early lapse will seem light indeed compared to the iniquity of the selfishness that has hidden it.

But *is* it selfishness that has hidden it? May it not be the conviction, shared but now by Honor herself, that in giving him freedom she would give him death—death moral, if not physical? May it not be her love, not her self-regard, that is closing her lips? How *could* she tell him? How could any mother tell any son? And how infinitely less possible would it be to a mother so high throned? *Tell him!* In what words could she convey such a fact? How could she make him believe it? If she were ever to brace herself to the awful rack of that confession, of what use would it be? She could never gain credence from him. He would think that her poor brain had turned through pity for his sufferings, and would draw over her sick fancies a veil of reverent tenderness. And if by some miracle she did get him to believe it?

The girl covers her face with both hands. Till now, absorbed in the immensity of her pity for the man she loves, she has felt nothing but unspeakable indignation against the author of his destruction ; but now an ocean of compassion for that most wretched author more wholesomely floods her being.

What must that woman have been suffering during these last days! What plowshares must have been furrowing her heart! What a hell of oscillation between two terrific alternatives! What a choice of cups to have to offer him to drink—the incurable blight of madness, or the defilement of all the sanctities of his past! Honor feels that it is only in part that she can realize what the tortures must be of a mind held by the seventy-and-seven devils of such an occupancy. But the mere partial grasp of it tears groans of pity, in which her own grief has now no part, out of her heart.

"You poor, poor souls! God pity you both!"

She sits there huddled up, with her elbows on her knees, and her hands still covering her face, as if to hide out some blood-curdling sight, for hours. What difference can time make to her?

It is a very commonplace sound that at last arouses her to the consciousness that she must not spend the night out of doors, viz., the scolding notes of the blackbirds quarreling over their roosting-places, hustling each other away. She slowly lets fall her hands, and draws herself up, stiff and a little chilled, and the light, running level now under the tree boughs from its parent fount in the green and scarlet west, makes her long-shielded eyes blink. The blackbirds' altercation pauses for a moment, and there is no sound but the voice of a harsh jay, ugly and unmusical, drowning, save to her practiced ear, the voice of a little tree creeper.

"God pity us all!" she says out loud.

CHAPTER XVII.

A BURDEN is always a burden, but it may be so adjusted as to be carried with upright head instead of staggered under with bowed back.

By the time of his return to England, in latish October, Harry Clarence has learned how to carry his. It is still there,—nay, it has not lost one ounce of its weight,—but he has at least begun to teach himself the lesson of how it should be carried. The heavenly winged love that had hovered for a brief space on his life's threshold has forever flitted away, but he has ceased to send unmanly crying and groans after her, bowing his head in acknowledgment that she was too fair for him, and acquiescing in her return to her home in the skies. The phantom of insanity still dogs him; but he has taken the ugly thing by the throat, and defied it. The horrid visions that encumbered his sleep have withdrawn, chased by the wholesome influences of change and travel and healthy fatigue. He has learned not to blench from the contemplation of his losses, but rather to reckon up with quiet fortitude what is left him.

Happiness is gone—in its supremest form of requited love irrecoverably departed. But work and duty remain; and there are worse things with which to fill our little life space, as he with patient courage tells himself. Out of unusual misfortunes great careers have ere now been forced, and though there are none of the elements of greatness in him, yet even he, handicapped as he is, can still walk worthily, as one forever ennobled by that refused and foregone love should do.

But it is not always that he can keep at this high level. He has failings of the spirit, against which, when they come upon him, for a while he struggles in vain. It is mostly at the sight of some common homely happiness that they attack him—some quiet, humdrum Sunday couple, innocent of anything in themselves or their circumstances that can make an agony of envy in another's breast, of some little jolly, rollicking child.

At such moments there is nothing for it but to grapple his mind with all its will-force to the recalling of what is still left him; of that perfect saintly love that has enveloped all his existence in its warm white folds. His mother! He can never have to renounce her. Nothing but death can deprive him of her. And she will not die; she will

"Absent herself from felicity awhile,"

knowing that he cannot do without her. His heart is overflowing with tenderness toward her as he nears the little railway station, which is within a mile of that rustic retreat to which she has cleaved during all the time of his absence.

His heart is full of tenderness, but there are also misgivings in it—misgivings, but not as to her physical welfare, for she has written regularly and calmly to each address he has given her. Besides, a good dependable lady's maid—not a friend, for Mrs. Clarence has always shrunk from making friends of her servants, but a trustworthy, conscientious person —would have kept him informed of any alteration in her health.

The misgivings he feels are as to the state of her spirits. Shall he find her, who, unlike himself, has not been subject to the wholesome bracing of change and travel, who has been confined to one scene, one very narrow set of surroundings, in the same condition of morbid prostration as he had left her in?

The wretched irritation which, in the miserable days before his departure, had assailed him at the sight of her hopeless gloom recurs, in some degree, at the recollection of it. If it is,—God forbid that it should be! but if it is so, he must—it will be his plain duty—use stringent measures to her; point out to her, with no mincing of his words, how impossible life will be to them both if she does not brace herself to a resolute effort to be cheerful.

He will show her—most lovingly, indeed, but so clearly and firmly that there may be no misapprehension—the unkindness to himself involved in her indulgence of such immoderate despondency; and he will show her, too, how, by her want of confidence in his goodness, she is discrediting that God upon whom, up to this last most crucial trial of her faith, she has so steadfastly leaned.

Clarence walks up the short distance from the station, tempted by the splendor of the autumn evening. Yet, though he has resolved to deal roundly with her if she disappoints him in the matter of recovered spirits and recuperated moral energy, he is in true haste to embrace her. And the admonishing impulse dies down, extinguished by pure love, as he comes in sight of the peaceful homestead, sitting in a gold bath of evening mist on the burned umber of its heath.

The gate where he had seen her lean to bid him good-by quickens yet more the hurry of heart to be reunited to her—to hear her soft cry of "Harry!" For has not he, in his haste, skipped the last pausing-place, and arrived twenty-four hours before he is due?

He is up the straight footpath, bordered by tall autumn flowers, with which the season, late as it is, has dealt leniently, and his hand is on the old-fashioned knocker of the, as he knows, never locked front door. You have only to give one turn to the bright brass, and there you are inside.

With an almost childish fear of being balked of the treat he promises himself in the sight of her glad astonishment, he almost runs up the flagged passage, and rather noisily, in his impatience, opens the door of the little parlor, to which, despite her listless lack of interest in anything, the habits and instincts of a lifetime have made her, by her daintiness and fragrances, give a delicate drawing room air.

As he enters, the perfume of her familiar dried rose leaves and lavender greets him, with its welcoming associations. His look flies at once to the long, low chair, lying in which he has seen her pass so many dejected hours. It is empty; and a flash of mixed disappointment and satisfaction darts across him—disappointment that their meeting may be deferred by her being out walking, and pleasure at the thought of its being an evidence of increased activity.

The light is drooping rapidly, and at first the room seems empty; but a second quick look around shows him that she is here, after all. In a little nook of the room stands a bureau, at which she writes her letters. It was his present to her on her last birthday; and at it she is sitting, with her back to him. She is not writing, but her head is lying on her outstretched arms in an attitude of the deepest despondency.

She is no better, then, than when he left her—giving the reins to the same indulgence in senseless despair as ever; not the same, indeed, but a more complete one, for scarcely ever before has he seen her in a pose of such utter abandonment.

The irritation that had been put out by love flares up again, and there is remonstrance mixed with the pained tenderness of his voice:

"*Mother!*"

But she does not stir. In a second he is at her side. Her face is quite hidden. He can see only the familiar coil upon coil of her splendid hair; and just beyond her prone head a letter lying, addressed to himself, and with the ink scarce dry upon the envelope.

Why should she be writing to him when she expects to see him in twenty-four hours? The thought does not occupy the millionth part of a minute.

"*Mother!* MOTHER!"

He has her in his arms; he has carried her to the window; has thrown it wide that the air may blow upon her face; has called madly for help.

The little room is full in a second. She is laid on the floor, and water dashed in her face. They beat her hands, and try to pour brandy down her throat.

"*Mother! mother!*"

But her son may leave his vain calling. Little as we know of the mystery that envelops the state of the dead—perhaps God has hidden it from us because, did we know the excellency of their estate, we should be in too mad haste to overtake them—little as we know of that deep mystery, I think we may be pretty sure that, even at his voice, she would not have come back if she could. Why should she come back? Is not her work done?

. . . . .

"Syncope, resulting from failure of the heart's action. An old-standing cardiac affection; the end precipitated possibly by some mental shock"—this with a look of interrogation. The usual medical patter upon a sudden death. "Life must have been extinct about half an hour at the time of his [the doctor's] arrival."

Half an hour! Then, if her son had driven up from the station, instead of walking, he would have found her still alive! This is one of those superfluous agonies that often add their tributary streams to the main river of a colossal grief.

But at present he feels no agony. Decorously

listening, it strikes him with a curious dry, hard sense of having been an unfortunate circumstance relating to the death of some stranger woman. He listens with the same cast-iron attention to the weeping narratives, interspersed with encomiums, of the lady's maid and the housewife.

"Oh, she *was* a good lady! Scarcely ever off her knees of late, and never missed a service at church! As regularly as the bell went, off she would go; though you might see that she could scarcely keep herself on her legs sometimes."

To his consciousness there seems to come a cold knowledge that, had this dead woman been akin to him, he would have been glad that she had made her way back to the well-head of waters which had fed her soul through life, and which, ere his departure, had seemed to have run dry.

"And charitable!"—this is the antiphonal strain—"and never giving any trouble! No lady—nor gentleman either, for the matter of that—who had ever crossed the threshold gave so little! And never caring what she ate!—eating no more than a sparrow!" etc., etc.

He has carried her upstairs ere this, and then returned to the sitting room, where by and by his would-be comforters leave him alone, he saying nothing either to detain or dismiss them.

When they are gone he begins to walk up and down, up and down, vaguely wishing that he could feel something, while around him the quick-coming night falls and falls. By and by they bring him in a lamp and tea. He thanks them civilly, and as civilly rebuts their good-natured insistence with him that he shall eat and drink.

When he is once again alone his eye falls on the letter still lying on the bureau,—the letter addressed to himself,—which the dusk has till now hidden from him, and which, in the *stun* of his mind, he had forgotten.

He takes it up, and at the sight of her handwriting the almost impenetrable veil of mist which shrouds him from sensation seems to lift a little, and he knows, for a second, that beyond that veil is intolerable pain.

The curtain falls again, and the pain goes. He stands holding the letter unopened in his hand, not even breaking the seal. Contrary to her custom, as he feels with a dull surprise, she has sealed it. What can she have to say to him that needs the safeguard of a seal?

He turns it over, and looks again at the superscription, then afresh at the impression on the seal—a little winged Justice, with scales. In infancy he has often played with that seal, and idly remembers having asked her the meaning of the figure. Still he does not open it, but stands as one doubtful and mazed.

After a while he takes a resolution: he will read it in her presence. Then, if there is anything in it hard to be understood, she will interpret. He listens; the house is quite quiet. His eye falls on the clock. She has been dead for three hours.

He takes the lamp, and steals noiselessly up the stairs to her door. The key is in it, and he enters. The frost is hard again about his heart, and the sight of the sheeted bed does not at first dissolve it. It seems to have no connection with his mother.

He sets down the lamp on the table near by, which is piled with her books of devotion. How many they are! From how many minds has she sought rest for her soul—that white angel-soul, fit in its perfect purity to rebuke the teachers at whose feet she has so meekly sat!

He has stepped to the bedside, and reverently turned down the sheet, a sort of odd disbelief in her being there at all mingling with his cold certainty of knowledge that she is. He looks steadfastly at her for a moment or two—looks at her lying there beautiful and happy, as the newly dead are wont to look, even those who in life have been unbeautiful and wretched. How much more she, that was ever so fair!

The next thing that he is conscious of is that he is lying groveling on the floor beside her bed, having returned to the lisping accents of infancy, and crying, "Mammy! mammy!"

The frost has broken, and he thinks that, in all God's quiver, there can be no more smarting shaft than that with which he is now piercing him. But before the night is over he knows better.

· · · · ·

The morning has dawned. Through the night none has disturbed the man's vigil. It has filled the sympathizing household with admiring pity that he should have had the will to keep it; but when the sun—late enough now in leaving his bed—has risen well above the heath, and has topped the church steeple, it seems to them strange that the watcher should not issue from the room.

By and by they have to summon him upon some necessary business connected with the funeral arrangements. They go, two together—for a sort of chilly dread is upon their spirits—the farmer's wife and the lady's maid, and try the door. It is locked on the inside, and the first two low knocks for admittance produce no result. At the third the key turns, the door opens, and Clarence stands before them. Both women start back with a low cry.

"God bless me, sir! I should not have known you!"

. . . . .

"He *do* take it hard, poor fellow!" is the later comment of the mistress of the house. "His hair turned like that all in one night? But I *do* wonder that he should have burned his ma's last letter—the very last she ever wrote him."

"And she that treasured up every scrap he had ever wrote her!" rejoins the maid, in watery antistrophe.

"He *must* have done it, though," rejoins the other, "for Sally found the *h*ashes, and she says she is confident there was not a mite of anything when she did up the grate yesterday; and he 'ad it in his 'and as he went upstairs last night, for I was watching him through the chink of the kitchen door."

They are right. In the silence of the dark hours, watching with her through her first night of death, he has burned the last letter she can ever write him. For in that letter she has made her expiation—the expiation which has cost her her life.

CHAPTER XVIII.

The autumn and winter go heavily by with Honor Lisle. They have been spent wholly at her dreary apology for a home, since her mainstay in friendship, Mrs. Bevis, has gone on a trip to America, and her other friends are few. Even if they were many, the total lack of pin-money in which her father keeps her would prevent her paying any visits that required even a modest amount of toilet.

Her loneliness is more complete than ever, since at the end of September her old nurse had died. There had been a sense of something painful come between them since the relation made by Mrs. Nasmyth; but the girl nurses her tenderly, and mourns her truly.

As she walks back across the park after the funeral, the darkness of her spirit is deepened by the knowledge that now one of the two channels through which freedom from the burden of apprehension under which he must stagger through life can come to him whom she loves is forever stopped. And yet God knows she dare not wish that he may ever learn.

A month later, when the park, unlike its poor little mistress, has put on the majesty of its gold and scarlet robes, she reads in the papers the announcement of Mrs. Clarence's death. For an hour she sits stunned. She is gone, then, carrying her secret out of the world, saving her good name, and not even having the courage to stay and help him to endure that life which her selfishness has made a hell.

But this mood, fiercely bitter while it lasts, soon yields to one of immense compassion. She is dead! It has killed her, and no wonder. Recalling the slight form and small lily face, she accompanies the dead in thought, with awed pity, through the stages of her Calvary, down the steps of her agonized descent to the grave, and, stirred to the depths of a naturally most pitiful heart, she breaks into long sobs and scalding tears. Yet as time goes on she realizes, by the added despondency of her own spirit, how much secret hope she must have nourished that her love might have received his release—awful as the suffering accompanying that release would have been—from the hand that can now never manumit him.

And as the shortening days march past in ever-darkening procession, a horrid temptation assails her. It is in *her* power alone now to redeem him. Why should not she do it? Her soul never willingly entertains the ugly guest, yet it comes back and back—sometimes in its native hideousness, sometimes tricked out mockingly like a duty. It comes back and back at intervals through the winter,—the enormous black winter,—with its innumerous hours of candlelight, when not even an Honor Lisle can be out of doors. She fights it with all the weapons in her armory—with eager work for bird and beast and poor neighbor, with uncongenial occupation of distasteful book and uphill study, and lastly with frightened, insistent prayer.

But even when February ushers in her lengthening days, snowdrop betrimmed, it is not wholly subdued. It is pushing her hard one morning toward the middle of the month, when all the twenty-two kinds of birds in her bower oak are making ready for their bridals, with epithalamiums as melodious as Spenser's. She is glad when the opening door, disclosing the young woman who has taken Mrs. Nasmyth's place as her attendant, effects a momentary diversion to the tyranny of her thought.

"If you please, 'm, there is a gentleman in the blue saloon that wishes to know if he could speak to you."

"A gentleman? what sort of a gentleman?"

The words are steady and quiet, but a Bedlamite hope is making the heart behind them curvet and bound.

"I could not say very well, 'm, for only one of the windows was unshuttered; but I should say he is an elderly sort of gentleman—his hair is quite gray."

The Bedlamite hope goes out, and in its extinction is recognized as having been Bedlamite.

"You had better ask him what he wants; I suppose he is someone on business from Tranby."

She says it with a sinking heart. It is probably one of the too-assiduous duns whom her father leaves her to grapple with.

"Oh, no, 'm,"—warmly,—"he is quite the gentleman."

"You should say quite *a* gentleman, not quite *the* gentleman, Martha"—the new attendant is a raw girl whom Honor is conscientiously trying to train. "Stay, I had better speak to him myself."

Her opinion of her maid's perspicacity is not high enough to lessen her confidence in the probable character of the visitor, and it is with the familiar sense of trepidating shame that she enters the blue saloon, and makes her way through its sea of brown-holland to the one unshuttered window.

The stranger is standing with his back to her, looking out. He is dressed in black. He has a slight stoop from the shoulders—yes, he must be an elderly man. Then he turns, and for a whole long minute there is dead silence. Is it possible that this is *he?*

"I have been ill," he says, in a voice which she finds it as difficult to piece on to her memory of him as she has already done in the case of his looks.

"Yes."

Another full minute of total dumbness; but the paralysis that had nailed her to the spot when she first stayed her steps is slackening its hold. She is stealing nearer, nearer to him. She is quite close to him now, her riveted eyes fastened on his stricken face—stricken, smitten, furrowed by plowshares of agony—and she knows that he knows!

Aged, broken, sunken-eyed, shrunk, and with blanched head, God has given him back to her!

She raises her arms, and her hands steal most softly to his bowed shoulders, and thence to his face, which, with tender compulsion, she draws down to hers.

"Hast thou any mind of me?"

His head falls forward on her neck, and with a storm of life-giving tears his answer comes:

"I have even great mind of thee!"

It is the only explanation they ever have.

THE END.

APPLETONS' TOWN AND COUNTRY LIBRARY.

PUBLISHED SEMIMONTHLY.

1. *The Steel Hammer.* By LOUIS ULBACH.
2. *Eve.* A Novel. By S. BARING-GOULD.
3. *For Fifteen Years.* A Sequel to The Steel Hammer. By LOUIS ULBACH.
4. *A Counsel of Perfection.* A Novel. By LUCAS MALET.
5. *The Deemster.* A Romance. By HALL CAINE.
6. *A Virginia Inheritance.* By EDMUND PENDLETON.
7. *Ninette:* An Idyll of Provence. By the author of Véra.
8. *"The Right Honourable."* By JUSTIN MCCARTHY and Mrs. CAMPBELL-PRAED.
9. *The Silence of Dean Maitland.* By MAXWELL GRAY.
10. *Mrs. Lorimer:* A Study in Black and White. By LUCAS MALET.
11. *The Elect Lady.* By GEORGE MACDONALD.
12. *The Mystery of the "Ocean Star."* By W. CLARK RUSSELL.
13. *Aristocracy.* A Novel.
14. *A Recoiling Vengeance.* By FRANK BARRETT. With Illustrations.
15. *The Secret of Fontaine-la-Croix.* By MARGARET FIELD.
16. *The Master of Rathkelly.* By HAWLEY SMART.
17. *Donovan:* A Modern Englishman. By EDNA LYALL.
18. *This Mortal Coil.* By GRANT ALLEN.
19. *A Fair Emigrant.* By ROSA MULHOLLAND.
20. *The Apostate.* By ERNEST DAUDET.
21. *Raleigh Westgate;* or, Epimenides in Maine. By HELEN KENDRICK JOHNSON.
22. *Arius the Libyan:* A Romance of the Primitive Church.
23. *Constance, and Calbot's Rival.* By JULIAN HAWTHORNE.
24. *We Two.* By EDNA LYALL.
25. *A Dreamer of Dreams.* By the author of Thoth.
26. *The Ladies' Gallery.* By JUSTIN MCCARTHY and Mrs. CAMPBELL-PRAED.
27. *The Reproach of Annesley.* By MAXWELL GRAY.
28. *Near to Happiness.*
29. *In the Wire-Grass.* By LOUIS PENDLETON.
30. *Lace.* A Berlin Romance. By PAUL LINDAU.
31. *American Coin.* A Novel. By the author of Aristocracy.
32. *Won by Waiting.* By EDNA LYALL.
33. *The Story of Helen Davenant.* By VIOLET FANE.
34. *The Light of Her Countenance.* By H. H. BOYESEN.
35. *Mistress Beatrice Cope.* By M. E. LE CLERC.
36. *The Knight-Errant.* By EDNA LYALL.
37. *In the Golden Days.* By EDNA LYALL.
38. *Giraldi;* or, The Curse of Love. By ROSS GEORGE DERING.
39. *A Hardy Norseman.* By EDNA LYALL.
40. *The Romance of Jenny Harlowe,* and *Sketches of Maritime Life.* By W. CLARK RUSSELL.
41. *Passion's Slave.* By RICHARD ASHE-KING.
42. *The Awakening of Mary Fenwick.* By BEATRICE WHITBY.
43. *Countess Loreley.* Translated from the German of RUDOLF MENGER.
44. *Blind Love.* By WILKIE COLLINS.
45. *The Dean's Daughter.* By SOPHIE F. F. VEITCH.
46. *Countess Irene.* A Romance of Austrian Life. By J. FOGERTY.
47. *Robert Browning's Principal Shorter Poems.*
48. *Frozen Hearts.* By G. WEBB APPLETON.
49. *Djambek the Georgian.* By A. G. VON SUTTNER.
50. *The Craze of Christian Engelhart.* By HENRY FAULKNER DARNELL.
51. *Lal.* By WILLIAM A. HAMMOND, M. D.
52. *Aline* A Novel. By HENRY GRÉVILLE.
53. *Joost Avelingh.* A Dutch Story. By MAARTEN MAARTENS.
54. *Katy of Catoctin.* By GEORGE ALFRED TOWNSEND.
55. *Throckmorton.* A Novel. By MOLLY ELLIOT SEAWELL.
56. *Expatriation.* By the author of Aristocracy.
57. *Geoffrey Hampstead.* By T. S. JARVIS.

APPLETONS' TOWN AND COUNTRY LIBRARY.—(*Continued.*)

58. *Dmitri.* A Romance of Old Russia. By F. W. BAIN, M. A.
59. *Part of the Property.* By BEATRICE WHITBY.
60. *Bismarck in Private Life.* By a Fellow-Student.
61. *In Low Relief.* By MORLEY ROBERTS.
62. *The Canadians of Old.* A Historical Romance. By PHILIPPE GASPÉ.
63. *A Squire of Low Degree.* By LILY A. LONG.
64. *A Fluttered Dovecote.* By GEORGE MANVILLE FENN.
65. *The Nugents of Carriconna.* An Irish Story. By TIGHE HOPKINS.
66. *A Sensitive Plant.* By E. and D. GERARD.
67. *Doña Luz.* By JUAN VALERA. Translated by Mrs. MARY J. SERRANO.
68. *Pepita Ximenez.* By JUAN VALERA. Translated by Mrs. MARY J. SERRANO.
69. *The Primes and their Neighbors.* By RICHARD MALCOLM JOHNSTON.
70. *The Iron Game.* By HENRY F. KEENAN.
71. *Stories of Old New Spain.* By THOMAS A. JANVIER.
72. *The Maid of Honor.* By Hon. LEWIS WINGFIELD.
73. *In the Heart of the Storm.* By MAXWELL GRAY.
74. *Consequences.* By EGERTON CASTLE.
75. *The Three Miss Kings.* By ADA CAMBRIDGE.
76. *A Matter of Skill.* By BEATRICE WHITBY.
77. *Maid Marian, and other Stories.* By MOLLY ELLIOT SEAWELL.
78. *One Woman's Way.* By EDMUND PENDLETON.
79. *A Merciful Divorce.* By F. W. MAUDE.
80. *Stephen Ellicott's Daughter.* By Mrs. J. H. NEEDELL.
81. *One Reason Why.* By BEATRICE WHITBY.
82. *The Tragedy of Ida Noble.* By W. CLARK RUSSELL.
83. *The Johnstown Stage, and other Stories.* By ROBERT H. FLETCHER.
84. *A Widower Indeed.* By RHODA BROUGHTON and ELIZABETH BISLAND.
85. *The Flight of the Shadow.* By GEORGE MACDONALD.
86. *Love or Money.* By KATHARINE LEE.
87. *Not All in Vain.* By ADA CAMBRIDGE.
88. *It Happened Yesterday.* By FREDERICK MARSHALL.
89. *My Guardian.* By ADA CAMBRIDGE.
90. *The Story of Philip Methuen.* By Mrs. J. H. NEEDELL.
91. *Amethyst:* The Story of a Beauty. By CHRISTABEL R. COLERIDGE.
92. *Don Braulio.* By JUAN VALERA. Translated by CLARA BELL.
93. *The Chronicles of Mr. Bill Williams.* By RICHARD MALCOLM JOHNSTON
94. *A Queen of Curds and Cream.* By DOROTHEA GERARD.
95. *"La Bella" and Others.* By EGERTON CASTLE.
96. *"December Roses."* By Mrs. CAMPBELL-PRAED.
97. *Jean de Kerdren.* By JEANNE SCHULTZ.
98. *Etelka's Vow.* By DOROTHEA GERARD.
99. *Cross Currents.* By MARY A. DICKENS.
100. *His Life's Magnet.* By THEODORA ELMSLIE.
101. *Passing the Love of Women.* By Mrs. J. H. NEEDELL.
102. *In Old St. Stephen's.* By JEANIE DRAKE.
103. *The Berkeleys and their Neighbors.* By MOLLY ELLIOT SEAWELL
104. *Mona Maclean, Medical Student.* By GRAHAM TRAVERS.
105. *Mrs. Bligh.* By RHODA BROUGHTON.
106. *A Stumble on the Threshold.* By JAMES PAYN.
107. *Hanging Moss.* By PAUL LINDAU.
108. *A Comedy of Elopement.* By CHRISTIAN REID.
109. *In the Suntime of her Youth.* By BEATRICE WHITBY.
110. *Stories in Black and White.* By THOMAS HARDY and Others.
110½. *An Englishman in Paris.* Notes and Recollections.
111. *Commander Mendoza.* By JUAN VALERA.
112. *Dr. Paull's Theory.* By Mrs. A. M. DIEHL.
113. *Children of Destiny.* By MOLLY ELLIOT SEAWELL.
114. *A Little Minx.* By ADA CAMBRIDGE.
115. *Capt'n Davy's Honeymoon.* By HALL CAINE.
116. *The Voice of a Flower.* By E. GERARD.
117. *Singularly Deluded.* By SARAH GRAND.
118. *Suspected.* By LOUISA STRATENUS.
119. *Lucia, Hugh, and Another.* By Mrs. J. H. NEEDELL.
120. *The Tutor's Secret.* By VICTOR CHERBULIEZ.

APPLETONS' TOWN AND COUNTRY LIBRARY.—(Continued.)

121. *From the Five Rivers.* By Mrs. F. A. STEEL.
122. *An Innocent Impostor, and Other Stories.* By MAXWELL GRAY.
123. *Ideala.* By SARAH GRAND.
124. *A Comedy of Masks.* By ERNEST DOWSON and ARTHUR MOORE.
125. *Relics.* By FRANCES MACNAB.
126. *Dodo: A Detail of the Day.* By E. F. BENSON.
127. *A Woman of Forty.* By ESMÈ STUART.
128. *Diana Tempest.* By MARY CHOLMONDELEY.
129. *The Recipe for Diamonds.* By C. J. CUTCLIFFE HYNE.
130. *Christina Chard.* By Mrs. CAMPBELL-PRAED.
131. *A Gray Eye or So.* By FRANK FRANKFORT MOORE.
132. *Earlscourt.* By ALEXANDER ALLARDYCE.
133. *A Marriage Ceremony.* By ADA CAMBRIDGE.
134. *A Ward in Chancery.* By Mrs. ALEXANDER
135. *Lot 13.* By DOROTHEA GERARD.
136. *Our Manifold Nature.* By SARAH GRAND.
137. *A Costly Freak.* By MAXWELL GRAY.
138. *A Beginner.* By RHODA BROUGHTON.
139. *A Yellow Aster.* By Mrs. MANNINGTON CAFFYN ("IOTA").
140. *The Rubicon.* By E. F. BENSON.
141. *The Trespasser.* By GILBERT PARKER.
142. *The Rich Miss Riddell.* By DOROTHEA GERARD.
143. *Mary Fenwick's Daughter.* By BEATRICE WHITBY.
144. *Red Diamonds.* By JUSTIN MCCARTHY.
145. *A Daughter of Music.* By G. COLMORE.
146. *Outlaw and Lawmaker.* By Mrs. CAMPBELL-PRAED.
147. *Dr. Janet of Harley Street.* By ARABELLA KENEALY.
148. *George Mandeville's Husband.* By C. E. RAIMOND.
149. *Vashti and Esther.*
150. *Timar's Two Worlds.* By M. JOKAI.
151. *A Victim of Good Luck.* By W. E. NORRIS.
152. *The Trail of the Sword.* By GILBERT PARKER.
153. *A Mild Barbarian.* By EDGAR FAWCETT.
154. *The God in the Car.* By ANTHONY HOPE.
155. *Children of Circumstance.* By Mrs. M. CAFFYN ("IOTA").
156. *At the Gate of Samaria.* By WILLIAM J. LOCKE.
157. *The Justification of Andrew Lebrun.* By FRANK BARRETT.
158. *Dust and Laurels.* By MARY L. PENDERED.
159. *The Good Ship Mohock.* By W. CLARK RUSSELL.
160. *Noëmi.* By S. BARING-GOULD.
161. *The Honour of Savelli.* By S. LEVETT YEATS.
162. *Kitty's Engagement.* By FLORENCE WARDEN.
163. *The Mermaid.* By L. DOUGALL.
164. *An Arranged Marriage.* By DOROTHEA GERARD.
165. *Eve's Ransom.* By GEORGE GISSING.
166. *The Marriage of Esther.* By GUY BOOTHBY.
167. *Fidelis.* By ADA CAMBRIDGE.
168. *Into the Highways and Hedges.* By F. F. MONTRÉSOR.
169. *The Vengeance of James Vansittart.* By Mrs. J. H. NEEDELL.
170. *A Study in Prejudices.* By GEORGE PASTON.
171. *The Mistress of Quest.* By ADELINE SERGEANT.
172. *In the Year of Jubilee.* By GEORGE GISSING.
173. *In Old New England.* By HEZEKIAH BUTTERWORTH.
174. *Mrs. Musgrave—and Her Husband.* By RICHARD MARSH.
175. *Not Counting the Cost.* By TASMA.
176. *Out of Due Season.* By ADELINE SERGEANT.

Each, 12mo, paper cover, 50 cents; cloth, $1.00.

For sale by all booksellers; or will be sent by mail on receipt of price by the publishers.

New York: D. APPLETON & CO., 72 Fifth Avenue.

D. APPLETON & CO.'S PUBLICATIONS.

THE GODS, SOME MORTALS, AND LORD WICKENHAM. By JOHN OLIVER HOBBES. With Portrait. 12mo. Cloth, $1.50.

The author of "Some Emotions and a Moral" presents in this book her most ambitious work. She has written, not a study, nor a collection of epigrams, but a complete novel in which she has gone deeper and further than in any previous essay. Her brilliancy of thought and style is familiar, but her admirers will find a new force in the sustained power with which she has drawn some remarkable characters and worked out an impressive theme.

BOG-MYRTLE AND PEAT. By S. R. CROCKETT. Uniform with "The Lilac Sunbonnet." 12mo. Cloth, $1.50.

The idyllic charm of "The Lilac Sunbonnet" reappears in this fascinating picture of the quaint humor, the stern conviction, and the passing shadows of Scottish life. Mr. Crockett has made his place, and readers need no introduction to his work.

IN THE FIRE OF THE FORGE. A Romance of Old Nuremberg. By GEORG EBERS, author of "Cleopatra," "An Egyptian Princess," etc. In 2 vols. 16mo.

Dr. Ebers's new romance transports the reader to mediæval Nuremberg, and depicts life in the imperial free city at the commencement of the Hapsburg dynasty. Its pages glow with vivid pictures of the olden days of chivalry, and its characters are knights, nobles, monks, nuns, fair maidens, and the patrician merchants whose stately homes still lend their picturesque charm to the Nuremberg of to-day.

MAJESTY. A Novel. By LOUIS COUPERUS. Translated by A. TEIXEIRA DE MATTOS and ERNEST DOWSON. 12mo. Cloth, $1.00.

"No novelist whom we can call to mind has ever given the world such a masterpiece of royal portraiture as Louis Couperus's striking romance entitled 'Majesty.'"—*Philadelphia Record.*

"A very powerful and cleverly written romance."—*New York Times.*

MASTER AND MAN. By Count LEO TOLSTOY. 16mo. Cloth, 75 cents.

In its simplicity, force, and directness this new work of fiction by Tolstoy will take a high rank among his shorter tales. There is no insistence upon a moral, but the impression left by the tale is none the less profound.

THE ZEIT-GEIST. By L. DOUGALL, author of "The Mermaid," "Beggars All," etc. 16mo. Cloth, 75 cents.

Miss Dougall has written a charming and thoughtful story in "The Zeit-Geist" which will not be forgotten by the reader. Its suggestions are of peculiar interest at a time when the subjects touched upon are in so many minds.

New York: D. APPLETON & CO., 72 Fifth Avenue.

D. APPLETON & CO.'S PUBLICATIONS.

ROUND THE RED LAMP. By A. Conan Doyle, author of "The White Company," "The Adventures of Sherlock Holmes," "The Refugees," etc. 12mo. Cloth, $1.50.

The "Red Lamp," the trade-mark, as it were, of the English country practitioner's office, is the central point of these dramatic stories of professional life. There are no secrets for the surgeon, and, a surgeon himself as well as a novelist, the author has made a most artistic use of the motives and springs of action revealed to him in a field of which he is the master.

"A volume of bright, clever sketches, ... an array of facts and fancies of medical life, and contains some of the gifted author's best work."—*London Daily News.*

A FLASH OF SUMMER. By Mrs. W. K. Clifford, author of "Love Letters of a Worldly Woman," "Aunt Anne," etc. 12mo. Cloth, $1.50.

"The story is well written and interesting, the style is limpid and pure as fresh water, and is so artistically done that it is only a second thought that notices it."—*San Francisco Call.*

THE LILAC SUNBONNET. A Love Story. By S. R. Crockett, author of "The Stickit Minister," "The Raiders," etc. 12mo. Cloth, $1.50.

"A love story pure and simple, one of the old-fashioned, wholesome, sunshiny kind, with a pure-minded, sound-hearted hero, and a heroine who is merely a good and beautiful woman; and if any other love story half so sweet has been written this year it has escaped us."—*New York Times.*

MAELCHO. By the Hon. Emily Lawless, author of "Grania," "Hurrish," etc. 12mo. Cloth, $1.50.

"A paradox of literary genius. It is not a history, and yet has more of the stuff of history in it, more of the true national character and fate, than any historical monograph we know. It is not a novel, and yet fascinates us more than any novel."—*London Spectator.*

THE LAND OF THE SUN. Vistas Mexicanas. By Christian Reid, author of "The Land of the Sky," "A Comedy of Elopement," etc. Illustrated. 12mo. Cloth, $1.75.

In this picturesque travel romance the author of "The Land of the Sky" takes her characters from New Orleans to fascinating Mexican cities like Guanajuato, Zacatecas, Aguas Calientes, Guadalajara, and of course the City of Mexico. What they see and what they do are described in a vivacious style which renders the book most valuable to those who wish an interesting Mexican travel-book unencumbered with details, while the story as a story sustains the high reputation of this talented author.

New York: D. APPLETON & CO., 72 Fifth Avenue.

D. APPLETON & CO.'S PUBLICATIONS.

Books by Mrs. Everard Cotes (Sara Jeannette Duncan).

THE STORY OF SONNY SAHIB. Illustrated. 12mo. Cloth, $1.00.

This little romance of youthful heroism will fascinate older and younger readers alike. It is a story of the Indian Mutiny and the years which immediately followed.

VERNON'S AUNT. With many Illustrations. 12mo. Cloth, $1.25.

"One of the best and brightest stories of the period."—*Chicago Evening Post.*

"A most vivid and realistic impression of certain phases of life in India, and no one can read her vivacious chronicle without indulging in many a hearty laugh."—*Boston Beacon.*

A DAUGHTER OF TO-DAY. A Novel. 12mo. Cloth, $1.50.

"This novel is a strong and serious piece of work; one of a kind that is getting too rare in these days of universal crankiness."—*Boston Courier.*

"A new and capital story, full of quiet, happy touches of humor."—*Philadelphia Press.*

A SOCIAL DEPARTURE: How Orthodocia and I Went Round the World by Ourselves. With 111 Illustrations by F. H. Townsend. 12mo. Paper, 75 cents; cloth, $1.75.

"It is to be doubted whether another book can be found so thoroughly amusing from beginning to end."—*Boston Daily Advertiser.*

"A brighter, merrier, more entirely charming book would be, indeed, difficult to find."—*St. Louis Republic.*

AN AMERICAN GIRL IN LONDON. With 80 Illustrations by F. H. Townsend. 12mo. Paper, 75 cents; cloth, $1.50.

"So sprightly a book as this, on life in London as observed by an American, has never before been written."—*Philadelphia Bulletin.*

THE SIMPLE ADVENTURES OF A MEM-SAHIB. With 37 Illustrations by F. H. Townsend. 12mo. Cloth, $1.50.

"It is like traveling without leaving one's armchair to read it. Miss Duncan has the descriptive and narrative gift in large measure, and she brings vividly before us the street scenes, the interiors, the bewilderingly queer natives, the gayeties of the English colony."—*Philadelphia Telegraph.*

New York: D. APPLETON & CO., 72 Fifth Avenue.

D. APPLETON & CO.'S PUBLICATIONS.

BEATRICE WHITBY'S NOVELS.

THE AWAKENING OF MARY FENWICK. 12mo. Paper, 50 cents; cloth, $1.00.

"Miss Whitby is far above the average novelist. . . . This story is original without seeming ingenious, and powerful without being overdrawn."—*New York Commercial Advertiser.*

PART OF THE PROPERTY. 12mo. Paper, 50 cents; cloth, $1.00.

"The book is a thoroughly good one. The theme is the rebellion of a spirited girl against a match which has been arranged for her without her knowledge or consent. . . . It is refreshing to read a novel in which there is not a trace of slipshod work."—*London Spectator.*

A MATTER OF SKILL. 12mo. Paper, 50 cents; cloth, $1.00.

"A very charming love-story, whose heroine is drawn with original skill and beauty, and whom everybody will love for her splendid if very independent character."—*Boston Home Journal.*

ONE REASON WHY. 12mo. Paper, 50 cents; cloth, $1.00.

"A remarkably well-written story. . . . The author makes her people speak the language of every-day life, and a vigorous and attractive realism pervades the book."—*Boston Saturday Evening Gazette.*

IN THE SUNTIME OF HER YOUTH. 12mo. Paper, 50 cents; cloth, $1.00.

"The story has a refreshing air of novelty, and the people that figure in it are depicted with a vivacity and subtlety that are very attractive."—*Boston Beacon.*

MARY FENWICK'S DAUGHTER. 12mo. Paper, 50 cents; cloth, $1.00.

"A novel which will rank high among those of the present season."—*Boston Advertiser.*

ON THE LAKE OF LUCERNE, and other Stories. 16mo. Boards, with specially designed cover, 50 cents.

"Six short stories carefully and conscientiously finished, and told with the graceful ease of the practiced *raconteur*."—*Literary Digest.*

"Very dainty, not only in mechanical workmanship but in matter and manner."—*Boston Advertiser.*

New York: D. APPLETON & CO., 72 Fifth Avenue.

D. APPLETON & CO.'S PUBLICATIONS.

GILBERT PARKER'S BEST BOOKS.

"Mr. Parker has been named more than once, and in quarters of repute, 'the coming man.'"—LONDON LITERARY WORLD.

The Trail of the Sword.

Paper, 50 cents; cloth, $1.00.

Philadelphia Bulletin.

"Mr. Parker here adds to a reputation already wide, and anew demonstrates his power of pictorial portrayal and of strong dramatic situation and climax."

Pittsburg Times.

"The tale holds the reader's interest from first to last, for it is full of fire and spirit, abounding in incident, and marked by good character drawing."

The Trespasser.

Paper, 50 cents; cloth, $1.00.

The Critic.

"Interest, pith, force, and charm—Mr. Parker's new story possesses all these qualities. . . . Almost bare of synthetical decoration, his paragraphs are stirring because they are real. We read at times—as we have read the great masters of romance—breathlessly."

Boston Advertiser.

"Gilbert Parker writes a strong novel, but thus far this is his masterpiece. . . . It is one of the great novels of the year."

The Translation of a Savage.

Flexible cloth, 75 cents.

The Nation.

"A book which no one will be satisfied to put down until the end has been matter of certainty and assurance."

Boston Home Journal.

"A story of remarkable interest, originality, and ingenuity of construction."

London Daily News.

"The perusal of this romance will repay those who care for new and original types of character, and who are susceptible to the fascination of a fresh and vigorous style."

New York: D. APPLETON & CO., 72 Fifth Avenue.

D. APPLETON & CO.'S PUBLICATIONS.

NOVELS BY HALL CAINE.

THE MANXMAN. 12mo. Cloth, $1.50.

"A story of marvelous dramatic intensity, and in its ethical meaning has a force comparable only to Hawthorne's 'Scarlet Letter.'"—*Boston Beacon.*

"A work of power which is another stone added to the foundation of enduring fame to which Mr. Caine is yearly adding."—*Public Opinion.*

"A wonderfully strong study of character; a powerful analysis of those elements which go to make up the strength and weakness of a man, which are at fierce warfare within the same breast; contending against each other, as it were, the one to raise him to fame and power, the other to drag him down to degradation and shame. Never in the whole range of literature have we seen the struggle between these forces for supremacy over the man more powerfully, more realistically delineated than Mr. Caine pictures it."—*Boston Home Journal.*

THE DEEMSTER. A Romance of the Isle of Man. 12mo. Cloth, $1.50.

"Hall Caine has already given us some very strong and fine work, and 'The Deemster' is a story of unusual power. . . . Certain passages and chapters have an intensely dramatic grasp, and hold the fascinated reader with a force rarely excited nowadays in literature."—*The Critic.*

"One of the strongest novels which has appeared in many a day."—*San Francisco Chronicle.*

"Fascinates the mind like the gathering and bursting of a storm."—*Illustrated London News.*

"Deserves to be ranked among the remarkable novels of the day."—*Chicago Times.*

THE BONDMAN. New edition. 12mo. Cloth, $1.50.

"The welcome given to this story has cheered and touched me, but I am conscious that, to win a reception so warm, such a book must have had readers who brought to it as much as they took away. . . . I have called my story a saga, merely because it follows the epic method, and I must not claim for it at any point the weighty responsibility of history, or serious obligations to the world of fact. But it matters not to me what Icelanders may call 'The Bondman,' if they will honor me by reading it in the open-hearted spirit and with the free mind with which they are content to read of Grettir and of his fights with the Troll."—*From the Author's Preface.*

CAPT'N DAVY'S HONEYMOON. A Manx Yarn. 12mo. Paper, 50 cents; cloth, $1.00.

"A new departure by this author. Unlike his previous works, this little tale is almost wholly humorous, with, however, a current of pathos underneath. It is not always that an author can succeed equally well in tragedy and in comedy, but it looks as though Mr. Hall Caine would be one of the exceptions."—*London Literary World.*

"It is pleasant to meet the author of 'The Deemster' in a brightly humorous little story like this. . . . It shows the same observation of Manx character, and much of the same artistic skill."—*Philadelphia Times.*

New York: D. APPLETON & CO., 72 Fifth Avenue.

D. APPLETON & CO.'S PUBLICATIONS.

ADA CAMBRIDGE'S NOVELS.

FIDELIS. 12mo., Paper, 50 cents; cloth, $1.00.

The animated and always interesting stories of Ada Cambridge have obtained a well merited popularity. In some respects "Fidelis" is her most ambitious work, and it is safe to predict for it a marked success among readers of wholesome and entertaining fiction.

MY GUARDIAN. 12mo. Paper, 50 cents; cloth, $1.00.

"A story which will, from first to last, enlist the sympathies of the reader by its simplicity of style and fresh, genuine feeling. . . . The author is *au fait* at the delineation of character."—*Boston Transcript.*

"The *dénoûment* is all that the most ardent romance reader could desire."—*Chicago Evening Journal.*

THE THREE MISS KINGS. 12mo. Paper, 50 cents; cloth, $1.00.

"An exceedingly strong novel. It is an Australian story, teeming with a certain calmness of emotional power that finds expression in a continual outflow of living thought and feeling."—*Boston Times.*

"The story is told with great brilliancy, the character and society sketching is very charming, while delightful incidents and happy surprises abound. It is a triple lovestory, pure in tone, and of very high literary merit.'—*Chicago Herald.*

NOT ALL IN VAIN. 12mo. Paper, 50 cents; cloth, $1.00.

"A worthy companion to the best of the author's former efforts, and in some respects superior to any of them."—*Detroit Free Press.*

"Its surprises are as unexpected as Frank Stockton's, but they are the surprises that are met with so constantly in human experience. . . . A better story has not been published in many moons."—*Philadelphia Inquirer.*

A MARRIAGE CEREMONY. 12mo. Paper, 50 cents; cloth, $1.00.

"'A Marriage Ceremony' is highly original in conception, its action graceful though rapid, and its characters sparkling with that life and sprightliness that have made their author rank as a peer of delineators."—*Baltimore American.*

"This story by Ada Cambridge is one of her best, and to say that is to at once award it high praise."—*Boston Advertiser.*

"It is a pleasure to read this novel."—*London Athenæum.*

A LITTLE MINX. 12mo. Paper, 50 cents; cloth, $1.00.

"A thoroughly charming new novel, which is just the finest bit of work its author has yet accomplished."—*Baltimore American.*

"The character of the versatile, resilient heroine is especially cleverly drawn."—*New York Commercial Advertiser.*

New York: D. APPLETON & CO., 72 Fifth Avenue.

D. APPLETON & CO.'S PUBLICATIONS.

NOVELS BY MAARTEN MAARTENS.

THE GREATER GLORY. A Story of High Life. By MAARTEN MAARTENS, author of "God's Fool," "Joost Avelingh," etc. 12mo. Cloth, $1.50.

"Until the Appletons discovered the merits of Maarten Maartens, the foremost of Dutch novelists, it is doubtful if many American readers knew that there were Dutch novelists. His 'God's Fool' and 'Joost Avelingh' made for him an American reputation. To our mind this just published work of his is his best. . . . He is a master of epigram, an artist in description, a prophet in insight."—*Boston Advertiser.*

"It would take several columns to give any adequate idea of the superb way in which the Dutch novelist has developed his theme and wrought out one of the most impressive stories of the period. . . . It belongs to the small class of novels which one can not afford to neglect."—*San Francisco Chronicle.*

"Maarten Maartens stands head and shoulders above the average novelist of the day in intellectual subtlety and imaginative power."—*Boston Beacon.*

GOD'S FOOL. By MAARTEN MAARTENS. 12mo. Cloth, $1.50.

"Throughout there is an epigrammatic force which would make palatable a less interesting story of human lives or one less deftly told."—*London Saturday Review.*

"Perfectly easy, graceful, humorous. . . . The author's skill in character-drawing is undeniable."—*London Chronicle.*

"A remarkable work."—*New York Times.*

"Maarten Maartens has secured a firm footing in the eddies of current literature. . . . Pathos deepens into tragedy in the thrilling story of 'God's Fool.'"—*Philadelphia Ledger.*

"Its preface alone stamps the author as one of the leading English novelists of to-day."—*Boston Daily Advertiser.*

"The story is wonderfully brilliant. . . . The interest never lags; the style is realistic and intense; and there is a constantly underlying current of subtle humor. . . . It is, in short, a book which no student of modern literature should fail to read."—*Boston Times.*

"A story of remarkable interest and point."—*New York Observer.*

JOOST AVELINGH. By MAARTEN MAARTENS. 12mo. Cloth, $1.50.

"So unmistakably good as to induce the hope that an acquaintance with the Dutch literature of fiction may soon become more general among us."—*London Morning Post.*

"In scarcely any of the sensational novels of the day will the reader find more nature or more human nature."—*London Standard.*

"A novel of a very high type. At once strongly realistic and powerfully idealistic."—*London Literary World.*

"Full of local color and rich in quaint phraseology and suggestion."—*London Telegraph.*

"Maarten Maartens is a capital story-teller."—*Pall Mall Gazette.*

"Our English writers of fiction will have to look to their laurels."—*Birmingham Daily Post.*

New York: D. APPLETON & CO., 72 Fifth Avenue.

D. APPLETON & CO.'S PUBLICATIONS.

MANY INVENTIONS. By RUDYARD KIPLING. Containing fourteen stories, several of which are now published for the first time, and two poems. 12mo, 427 pages. Cloth, $1.50.

"The reader turns from its pages with the conviction that the author has no superior to-day in animated narrative and virility of style. He remains master of a power which none of his contemporaries approach him—the ability to select out of countless details the few vital ones which create the finished picture. He knows how, with a phrase or a word, to make you see his characters as he sees them, to make you feel the full meaning of a dramatic situation."—*New York Tribune.*

"'Many Inventions' will confirm Mr. Kipling's reputation. . . . We would cite with pleasure sentences from almost every page, and extract incidents from almost every story. But to what end? Here is the completest book that Mr. Kipling has yet given us in workmanship, the weightiest and most humane in breadth of view."—*Pall Mall Gazette.*

"Mr. Kipling's powers as a story-teller are evidently not diminishing. We advise everybody to buy 'Many Inventions,' and to profit by some of the best entertainment that modern fiction has to offer."—*New York Sun.*

"'Many Inventions' will be welcomed wherever the English language is spoken. . . . Every one of the stories bears the imprint of a master who conjures up incident as if by magic, and who portrays character, scenery, and feeling with an ease which is only exceeded by the boldness of force."—*Boston Globe.*

"The book will get and hold the closest attention of the reader."—*American Bookseller.*

"Mr. Rudyard Kipling's place in the world of letters is unique. He sits quite aloof and alone, the incomparable and inimitable master of the exquisitely fine art of short-story writing. Mr. Robert Louis Stevenson has perhaps written several tales which match the run of Mr. Kipling's work, but the best of Mr. Kipling's tales are matchless, and his latest collection, 'Many Inventions,' contains several such."—*Philadelphia Press.*

"Of late essays in fiction the work of Kipling can be compared to only three—Blackmore's 'Lorna Doone,' Stevenson's marvelous sketch of Villon in the 'New Arabian Nights,' and Thomas Hardy's 'Tess of the D'Urbervilles.' . . . It is probably owing to this extreme care that 'Many Inventions' is undoubtedly Mr. Kipling's best book."—*Chicago Post.*

"Mr. Kipling's style is too well known to American readers to require introduction, but it can scarcely be amiss to say there is not a story in this collection that does not more than repay a perusal of them all."—*Baltimore American.*

"As a writer of short stories Rudyard Kipling is a genius. He has had imitators, but they have not been successful in dimming the luster of his achievements by contrast. . . . 'Many Inventions' is the title. And they are inventions—entirely original in incident, ingenious in plot, and startling by their boldness and force."—*Rochester Herald.*

"How clever he is! This must always be the first thought on reading such a collection of Kipling's stories. Here is art—art of the most consummate sort. Compared with this, the stories of our brightest young writers become commonplace."—*New York Evangelist.*

"Taking the group as a whole, it may be said that the execution is up to his best in the past, while two or three sketches surpass in rounded strength and vividness of imagination anything else he has done."—*Hartford Courant.*

"Fifteen more extraordinary sketches, without a tinge of sensationalism, it would be hard to find. . . . Every one has an individuality of its own which fascinates the reader."—*Boston Times.*

New York: D. APPLETON & CO., 72 Fifth Avenue.

www.ingramcontent.com/pod-product-compliance
Lightning Source LLC
Chambersburg PA
CBHW032102230426
43672CB00009B/1607